I0109040

The Distinctive Characteristics of the Lutheran Church, with special reference to the Lutheran Church of America

G. LUECKE

ORIGINALLY PUBLISHED BY
ST. LOUIS, MO
CONCORDIA PUBLISHING HOUSE
1920
CONCORDIA SERIES
OF
MODERN LITERATURE
THEOLOGICAL AND RELIGIOUS

www.JustandSinner.com

THE DISTINCTIVE CHARACTERISTICS OF THE LUTHERAN CHURCH, WITH SPECIAL REFERENCE TO THE LUTHERAN CHURCH OF AMERICA

By G. Luecke

Copyright 2015 Just and Sinner. All rights reserved. The original text is in public domain, but regarding this updated edition, besides brief quotations, none of this book shall be reproduced without permission.
Permission inquiries may be sent to
JustandSinner@yahoo.com

Just & Sinner
425 East Lincoln Ave.
Watseka, IL 60970

www.JustandSinner.com

ISBN 10: 0692453466
ISBN 13: 978-0692453469

Prefatory Note

This treatise has been prepared in answer to a widespread demand for a handbook containing in concise form such information on the Lutheran Church as will be sought especially by laymen, both Lutheran and non-Lutheran, for the purpose of forming a better acquaintance with, and a correct judgment on, the Lutheran Church. The work, which was begun several years ago, but was retarded by ill health and other adverse circumstances, is now sent forth with the wish and prayer that it may lead Lutherans to a fuller appreciation of the glorious heritage of their Church, and that it may convince others of the claims which the Lutheran Church has upon their consideration.

G. LUECKE.

CONTENTS

Introduction

The Lutheran Church, the Church founded by, and taking its name from, Dr. Martin Luther, is not a new Church and does not teach a doctrine invented by its founder, but is the ancient Christian Church, repristinated and restored to its apostolic purity. For during the fifteen centuries that had intervened between the founding of the Church and its reformation by Luther, it had widely departed from this pristine purity of faith and morals and practice. Already in the time of the apostles "the mystery of iniquity did work" (2 Thess. 2:7), and "many false prophets had gone out into the world" (1 John 4:1). And things had gone from bad to worse in this respect in the course of time. During the first centuries the Church was rent by many divisions through the rise of false teachers, who frequently taught doctrines directly subversive of the very foundation of Christianity, gathering strong followings and working much damage to the cause of the Gospel. And finally there came the great "falling away," led by the Pope of Rome, that "man of sin, who opposes and exalts himself above all that is called God, or that is worshiped, so that he sits in the temple of God, showing himself that he is God" (2 Thess. 2:3, 4). What need to speak of the awful "abomination of desolation" (Matt. 24:15) which he had wrought in the holy place, the spiritual temple of Christ's holy Church, by his monstrous doctrines and abuses? What need of rehearsing the story of the tremendous task performed by the heroic Reformer in the cleansing of this "Augean stable" four hundred years ago? The blows of the hammer that nailed those ninety-five theses have reverberated throughout the whole world during all these centuries, and will continue to reecho through the ages, till the last trumpet sounds the knell of this world's existence, and time will be merged into the ceaseless ages of eternity.

Scarcely had the sound of Luther's hammer-blows died away, when the news began to spread like wildfire and to kindle a discussion throughout the length and breadth of Germany that shook the very foundations of the papal edifice, and finally wrested the greater part of its population from the dominion of Roman Catholic error and abuses.— This early spread was later, to some degree, counteracted by various causes, notably the dissensions and lamentable religious wars, that arose among the different Protestant factions, and the Roman Catholic counter-reformation. Especially was this the case in southern Germany, so that to this day this section is largely Catholic, while the northern part of the Empire is almost exclusively Protestant.

From Germany the Reformation spread to neighboring countries, to Bohemia, Switzerland, France, and the Netherlands. However, in most of these, notably the last-named three, Luther's doctrine was supplanted by that of the Swiss reformers, Calvin and Zwingli, and in one of them—France—Rome succeeded by bloody persecution in all but wiping out the Huguenots.— It is to be noted that the movement also in these countries, while marching under somewhat different colors, was a direct outgrowth of Luther's Reformation in Germany, as indeed all the Protestant church-bodies are offshoots of the Lutheran Church.

Among the countries into which the influence of Luther's Reformation at first extended, but where it was afterward nullified to a large extent by various causes, was also England. The soil had here been prepared for the reception of the seed by the work of Wyclif, the English "Morning-star of the Reformation." When Luther's powerful writings began to appear in print, they found eager students at the two great universities, first at Cambridge and later at Oxford. Tyndale's translation of the New Testament and, later, Coverdale's Bible were largely retranslations of Luther's German version, or at least closely dependent on it. Coverdale also translated Luther's hymns into English. In 1536 an English translation of the Augsburg Confession and Apology appeared. The X Articles were compiled from the Augsburg Confession, the Apology, and another treatise of Melanchthon. The *Bishops' Book* of 1537 also draws freely from Lutheran services. The XIII Articles, which formed the basis of the later XXXIX Articles, the Confession of the Anglican Church, were taken mostly from the Augsburg Confession. *The First Prayer-book* was so closely dependent on Lutheran liturgies that it has been classed among them. A commission of leading men was sent from England to Wittenberg in 1535 in order to reach an understanding with Luther and his colleagues, and a similar commission went from Germany to England in 1538 to continue the discussion.

The Lutheran movement in England was killed by King Henry VIII, an ambitious, lewd, and tyrannical ruler, for personal and political reasons. When the Lutheran doctrines first began to spread in his realm, Henry turned against Luther in a vicious attack, which earned him the title of "Defender of the Faith" from the Pope, and he proceeded to root out the Lutheran "heresy" with bloody and fiery persecution. When, however, the Pope failed to sanction immediately the desired annulment of Henry's first marriage to Catherine of Aragon, in order to enable him to wed Anne Boleyn, a lady of his court, with whom he had become enamored, Henry just as readily turned against the Pope, declaring the Church of England free from Rome and himself its head. The outcome was the Anglican Church, which by its retention of some Roman Catholic errors and abuses, its adoption of some Lutheran doctrines, and the later introduction of Reformed elements, is neither papal nor Lutheran nor Reformed, but a mixture of all three. But it still remains true what Nicholas Lithenius, Swedish pastor of a Lutheran congregation in London during the seventeenth century, stated in a book on this subject, to wit, "That Luther, the Great Instrument of God in Reforming the British Church, Opened the Way to

England and Scotland to Extricate Themselves from Papal Servitude."

While the early spread of the Reformation was largely checked in the South and West, this was not the case in the North, where it soon obtained entrance into the Scandinavian countries. Almost immediately it reached the neighboring country of Denmark, where it was introduced under Christian II and his successors, Frederick and Christian III, and soon became the State Church. From Denmark the Reformation was transplanted, a little later, to Norway, which was then under Danish rule. Its introduction here was accompanied by some violence, the Catholic bishops being deposed by force at the command of the Danish king and the Lutheran Church established by royal decree. Similarly the Reformation was forcibly introduced by the Danish king into Iceland, which still belongs to Denmark. In both these countries, therefore, the introduction of the new faith met at first with a good deal of opposition, but finally it achieved a complete triumph over Catholicism.

Into Sweden the Reformation was introduced directly from Germany, almost as early as into Denmark. Up to that time this country, too, had been under the sovereignty of the Danish king, but under the leadership of the famous Gustavus Vasa it achieved its independence, and Gustavus was chosen king in 1523. He early embraced the Lutheran faith, and through his personal influence Lutheranism was made the acknowledged religion of Sweden at the diet of Westeras in 1527. He thus became the liberator of his country both politically and religiously.—In all the Scandinavian countries

Lutheranism has continued to retain an almost universal hold to this day, so that all other church-bodies form but an insignificant and negligible part of their populations.—As these countries originally received the Reformation from Germany, so the development of their Lutheranism has been largely influenced by its development in Germany. For while the outward form of polity differs somewhat from that of the German Church,—*e. g.*, both the Swedish and the Finnish Lutheran Church have the episcopal form of government,—yet the Scandinavian churches have been successively swept by a wave of orthodoxy, pietism, and rationalism originating in Germany.

From Scandinavia Lutheranism was carried to the Finns and Lapps, as well as to the Eskimos of Greenland, all of whom are generally classed with the Mongolian race.—Into Finland and Lapland the Roman Catholic faith had been previously introduced, but with indifferent success, and at the time of the Reformation most of the people in both countries were practically pagans. Gustavus Vasa, of whose country Finland was then a province, promoted the spread of the Lutheran faith in that country, and succeeded in firmly establishing it there, so that the great majority of its inhabitants are Lutherans to-day. He also sought to introduce the Reformation among the Lapps in the northern part of Sweden, and his successors continued the work, which was of slow growth, owing to the great difficulties it encountered among this semi-barbarous and roving people. Also the Danes and the Norwegians, and later the Finns, have taken up the work among them and are vigorously prosecuting it to the present time.—From Norway the Lutheran faith was also carried to pagan Greenland during the first half of the eighteenth century. The pioneer in this work was Hans Egede, "the Apostle of Greenland." By his labors, continued by his son and other missionaries from Denmark that followed him, Greenland has, in the course of time, become thoroughly Christianized, and nearly all of its native Eskimos are now Lutherans.

Also to many parts of what was until recently the Empire of Russia the Lutheran faith was extended during the days of the Reformation or after. As early as 1529 Lutheran doctrine was preached in the Baltic provinces (Courland, Esthonia, Livonia), and the work was greatly promoted when these provinces came under Swedish control at the time of Gustavus Adolphus. Also into Russian Poland the Reformation was introduced at a very early period. In 1525 the first Lutheran preachers entered the country, and in 1565 a Lutheran synod was organized, and large Lutheran congregations existed there up to the outbreak of the present war. In other parts of the empire large Lutheran settlements were formed since Reformation times, *e. g.*, in St. Petersburg, Odessa, Bessarabia, the Crimea, in fact, in many parts of southern Russia, even in far-off Siberia, in Tobolsk, Tomsk, Omsk, Irkutsk, and Vladivostok.

In many other directions and to other continents did the Lutheran Church extend her missionary activity, as soon as she was firmly established at home. In 1634 the first missionary went from Germany to Abyssinia, and he was soon followed by others. Being driven from that country, they made their way down the eastern coast of Africa, and the outcome was the establishment of the East African missions, which now extend over almost the entire eastern part of the continent, and are now conducted by six different missionary societies.—Also in South and West Africa Lutheran missions were begun in the last century, as an outgrowth of German settlements there. The churches of Norway and Sweden also have mission-stations in Africa, but the chief mission-territory of the former is the island of Madagascar.—At the beginning of the eighteenth century Lutheran mission-work was begun in India by the great pioneer missionary Ziegenbalg, who, while himself a German, was sent there by the Danish king Frederick IV. At present, work in that country is carried on by a number of European mission societies and by several Lutheran synods of our own country. Other countries that have been entered by Lutheran missionaries are Brazil and Argentina in South America; Persia, China, and Japan in Asia; the islands south of Asia; Australia, New Zealand, and neighboring islands. Thus the Church of the Reformation has literally encompassed the globe. The numerical results of its work and its relative standing among the churches of the earth will appear in the following paragraphs of

Statistics: The Lutheran Church numbers, according to the latest, but indiscriminate compilations: in Europe, 58,106,319 adherents; in Asia, 355,580; in Africa, 384,566; in Oceania, 200,372; in South America, 622,000; in Central

America, about 1,000; in North America (inclusive of Mexico and Greenland), 11,730,016. This makes a total of 71,399,852 Lutherans for the entire globe. The figures of the other leading Protestant Churches, according to the latest available statistics (1916), are as follows: Methodists, 32,418,330; Presbyterian and Reformed, 30,799,854; Episcopalians, 26,758,267; Baptists, 21,002,211; Congregationalists, 4,355,172. This shows that the Lutheran Church is numerically at the head of the Protestant Churches in the world, having more than twice as many nominal adherents as any other one of them.

"Lutheran," then, this Church calls herself, after the name of her founder. And she is proud of that name! Not that she glories in the man Luther. For she did not choose the name herself, but it was foisted upon her by her enemies as a title of opprobrium, just as the name "Christian" was given to the early disciples by the heathen as an epithet of ridicule; and no one protested more vehemently against the name than Luther himself, saying that he would much rather that his followers should call themselves by the simple name of "Christians." But in spite of his protests the name given in derision to his followers has clung to them, and so to this day the Church that was founded by him bears the name as a title of honor, for the purpose of distinguishing itself from other erring Protestant church-bodies. Hence the objection of those falls to the ground who tell us that we have no right to bear the name of a man, but that we ought to call ourselves simply "Christians," after the name of the Savior.

Lutherans would be the first to discard their name and to return to the use of the original name alone, if the various denominations of Christendom were to return to the original Gospel-truth as preached by Christ and His apostles, and brought to light again by Dr. Martin Luther.

The chief characteristic of the true Lutheran Church ever since the days of its founder has been strict adherence to the Scriptures in all matters of faith and practice. That was the cardinal principle which actuated Luther in his great work of reforming the abuses in the Church, and which he upheld against the Romanists on the one hand and the Reformed theologians on the other. While the former set up the authority of councils and Popes, and the latter the authority of reason, as a guide in religion, his sole argument was, "It is written." And this has ever since been the guiding star of all truly Lutheran teaching and practice, and is such to-day. Hence the unflinching adherence of the Lutheran Church to purity of doctrine and practice and its uncompromising attitude towards all forms of error and its opposition to the laxity in faith as well as practice, which is so common in our day and country. For this attitude Lutherans are often decried as bigoted and narrow-minded. But it is the "bigotry" and "narrow-mindedness" of the Word of God itself! Therefore, in such matters as God in His Word has left free, Lutherans are very "broad," refusing to be bound by any ordinances or teachings of men, and the greatest liberty in these non-essentials prevails among them. Because Luther was guided by this principle in his reformatory work, he retained many ceremonies and customs that he found in the Catholic Church, as they are neither commanded nor forbidden in the Bible, and could therefore be retained without injury, while their wholesale abolition might only tend to create disturbance and confusion, as was shown in the case of Muentzer and the other "heavenly prophets." His was therefore rightly called the "Conservative Reformation." And thus to this day certain of these externals prevail in Lutheran churches which are sometimes considered "Catholic" by people of other churches, and even by ill-informed Lutherans themselves.

It is the purpose of the following pages, as already intimated in the Preface, to discuss the main characteristic features of the Lutheran Church that distinguish her from other churches, so as to enable candid inquirers into religious truth to judge of her merits and to determine for themselves whether they ought to unite with her in preference to some other Church; and at the same time to give to Lutherans themselves a handbook of information about their Church, that will make them better able to defend her against the attacks of opponents, lead them to a fuller realization of her claim upon their allegiance, and inspire them with a greater love for her principles and institutions.

> My Church! my Church! my dear old
>   Church!
> My fathers' and my own!
> On prophets and apostles built,
> And Christ the Corner-stone!
> All else beside, by storm or tide,
> May yet be overthrown;

But not my Church—my dear old Church—
My fathers' and my own!

My Church! my Church! my dear old
    Church!
My glory and my pride!
Firm in the faith Immanuel taught,
She holds no faith beside.
Upon this rock, 'gainst every shock,
Though gates of hell assail,
She stands secure, with promise sure:
"They never shall prevail."

My Church! my Church! I love my Church,
For she exalts my Lord.
She speaks, she breathes, she teaches not
But from His written Word.
And if her voice bids me rejoice,
From all my sins released,
'Tis through th' atoning sacrifice,
And Jesus is the Priest.

PART I

Distinctive Doctrines of the Lutheran Church

The purpose of this book is to set forth the distinctive features of the Lutheran Church, *i. e.*, those features that distinguish it from other Churches. The purpose, therefore, of this section will be to point out those doctrines which the Lutheran Church holds in distinction from other Churches. The aim will not be, accordingly, to give a complete analysis of the Lutheran system of doctrine, and the reader will look in vain for the discussion of doctrines that the great body of Christians hold in common, such as the doctrine of the Trinity, of prayer, and others. Manifestly it would also be impossible, within the scope of a popular treatise such as this is designed to be, to treat *all* the minor differences between our Church and others; on the contrary, we shall have to confine ourselves to the more important doctrines forming the center of Christianity, to wit, those concerning more or less directly the great central theme of man's eternal salvation. Hence we take up first those doctrines connected with

THE WAY OF SALVATION

"What must I do to be saved?" this question of the trembling jailer at Philippi (Acts 16:30, 31) is the most vital and important question for every man to ask. For upon the right answer to this question depends his eternal destiny. And there is only one correct answer to this question. It is the one which Paul gave: "Believe on the Lord Jesus Christ, and thou shalt be saved." This answer contains, in a nutshell, all the elements of the way of salvation: the Lord Jesus Christ, the Redeemer of fallen sinful mankind, and the appropriation of His redemption by faith. The Lutheran position on the redemption of the world by Christ is the first point, accordingly, that we must discuss in this connection.

THE NECESSITY OF REDEMPTION

The Lutheran Church maintains, in accordance with the Scriptures, that *the utter sinfullness of the whole human race* necessitated a universal redemption. "There is no difference; for all have sinned and come short of the glory of God" (Rom. 3:23). Many other passages of similar import might be adduced (compare Eccl. 7:20; Prov. 20:9; Ps. 14:2, 3; 1 John 1:8; John 3:6), but this one is sufficient to prove the Scripturalness of the Lutheran view, *viz.*, that all men are sinners, and that on account of their sins they are lost and need redemption.

All men are sinners. What does that mean? That means according to the Scriptures that all men are by nature utterly corrupt, without a spark of good in their hearts, without the least power to do anything that is good in the sight of God. "That which is born of the flesh is flesh" (John 3:6), that is, every child born of human parents is corrupt in its nature. Compare Paul's words: "I know that in me, that is, in my flesh, dwells no good thing." (Rom. 7:18. Read the whole chapter!) And whence is this corruption? It was brought about by the fall of Adam and Eve, and has been transplanted from them through natural generation to all their descendants, i. e., the whole human race. (Compare Gen. 5:3. "And Adam ... begat a son in his own likeness, after his image," with John 3:6, quoted above.)—And out of this natural corruption of man's heart flow the actual sins, which he commits by thoughts, words, and deeds. "When lust has conceived, it brings forth sin" (Jas. 1:15). "Out of the heart" (the corrupt heart of man) "proceed evil thoughts: murders, adulteries, fornications, thefts, false witness, blasphemies" (Matt. 15:19). Thus it comes about that "there is no difference; for all have sinned, and come short of the glory of God" (Rom. 3:23).

This Scriptural view of the utter corruption and sinfulness of the entire human race the Lutheran Church holds fast over against the modern view entertained by many people in most of the other Protestant Churches, and often put forth both in the religious and secular press of the day, that man is not altogether bad by nature, that there is in every person an element of good; and that only some outward influence is required to bring out the good that is in him. And also in opposition to the more radical view, that every child is by nature good; that it learns to do wrong only from the evil examples of its surroundings; that, if you could place a child where all the influences would be good and ennobling, he would naturally grow up to be good. This view is contradicted not only by Scripture which says: "The imagination of man's heart is evil from his youth" (Gen. 8:21), but also by daily experience, which shows that little children are sinful long before they are influenced by evil example.

The Lutheran Church maintains, in harmony with the Scriptures, that on account of their natural depravity and sinfullness *all men are subject to God's wrath and liable to eternal punishment.* The Scriptures teach plainly that man's natural sinful condition already places him under God's wrath and punishment. "We were by nature the children of wrath, even as others" (Eph. 2:3). And in similar terms they speak of the resultant wickedness of men in words and acts. "The wrath of God is revealed from heaven against all ungodliness and unrighteousness of men, who hold the truth in unrighteousness." (Rom. 1:18. Read the rest of the chapter!) God cannot but be angry at sin and punish it, because He is a holy and righteous God. When He gave His holy Law on Mount Sinai, He added the solemn words: "I the Lord, thy God, am a jealous God, visiting the iniquity of the fathers upon the children unto the third and fourth generation of them that hate Me" (Ex. 20:5). And again we read: "The Lord, thy God, is a consuming fire, even a jealous God" (Deut. 4:24). And because His righteousness, which has been offended by man's sin, is an infinite righteousness,—for God is infinite in all His attributes,—therefore it also demands an infinite satisfaction and punishment for sin. And because man, a finite being, cannot render such a satisfaction of infinite value, he is doomed to a punishment infinite in extent. And so the verdict of the great Judge upon the wicked will be: "Depart from Me, ye cursed, into *everlasting* fire" (Matt. 25:41).

This is the Scriptural teaching concerning the justice of God and the punishment of sin. And this is, therefore, also the teaching of the Lutheran Church in contradistinction from the prevalent modern view, which, ignoring the justice of God, would have us believe that God, being a God of love, could certainly never condemn a single one of His creatures to endless torments and misery in the flames of hell; that, being an almighty God, He is "abundantly able to forgive sins without exacting any expiation for them." This modern view, which has permeated almost all Protestant Churches outside of the Lutheran to a larger or less degree, in the last analysis makes an atonement for sin and the redemption of the sinner unnecessary, while the Lutheran view, as set forth above, uncompromisingly maintains its necessity, if man is to escape the penalty of his sin which the justice of God demands. And so we come now to consider

THE REDEMPTION OF THE SINFUL HUMAN RACE

With reference to the person of the Redeemer the Lutheran Church maintains, on the basis of Scripture, the divine-human character of Jesus Christ.—It required a true man to redeem sinful man. Only a man could become the substitute, the representative of man in this work of meriting heaven for him. "Forasmuch, then, as the children are partakers of flesh and blood, He Himself likewise took part of the same, that through death He might destroy him that had the power of death, that is, the devil. For, verily, He took not on Him the nature of angels, but He took on Him the seed of Abraham" (Heb. 2:14, 15). For the fallen angels, the devils, there is no redemption, because Christ did not assume their nature, and so could not be their substitute and surety. He could redeem only the human race, because He became a man like unto us, sin excepted. Therefore, "when the fullness of the time was come, God sent forth His Son, *made of a woman*, made under the Law, to redeem them that were under the Law" (Gal. 4:4, 5).—"God sent forth *His Son*." The Redeemer is also true God. God "gave His *only-begotten Son*" (John 3:16); "God spared not *His own Son*" (Rom. 8:32). The son, the child, is always of the same nature with his father. The son of a human father can be no other than human; the Son of God, begotten of His essence, cannot but be divine. And so the Scriptures plainly and emphatically predicate of Christ that He is "the true God" (1 John 5:20); that He "is over all, God blessed forever" (Rom. 9:5).— And this, too, was necessary for our redemption. For no mere man, though he were perfect and sinless, could have accomplished this great work. For "none of them can by any means redeem his brother, nor give to God a ransom for him (for the redemption of their soul is precious, and it ceases forever) that he should still live and not see corruption" (Ps. 49:7, 8). With all the riches of earth a man could not buy exemption for his brother from temporal death: how, then, should he be able to redeem him from eternal death? And if he could not redeem one brother, how much less all the numberless human race! No, only "the blood of Jesus Christ, the *Son of God*, cleanses us from all sin" (1 John 1:7); only "Christ *the Lord*," i.e., Jehovah, the eternal, unchangeable God, could be the "Savior" (Luke 2:11). For the infinite justice of an infinite God, which had been outraged by sin, required an infinite satisfaction, and this no finite creature, such as man is,—this only an infinite being, only a being that was God Himself, was able to render.—Thus, then, a divine-human Savior, a Savior who was God and man *in one person*, was needed to redeem us: a human Savior, that He might be man's substitute; a divine Savior that His substitution might satisfy God. Thus it was, then, that "God sent forth His Son, made of a woman" (Gal. 4:4), that "the Word was made flesh" (John 1:14), that "God was manifest in the flesh" (1 Tim. 3:16). In Jesus Christ this double requisite was fulfilled; for in Him, the "Son of Man" (Matt. 18:11), "the man Christ Jesus" (1 Tim. 2:5), "dwells all the fullness of the Godhead bodily" (Col. 2:9).

This Scriptural doctrine of the person of our blessed Redeemer the Lutheran Church upholds, in the first place, against the gross error of Antitrinitarians, *i.e.*, of those who deny the Trinity of Persons in the Godhead, maintaining that there is only one God and only one divine Person, that therefore Jesus Christ cannot be true God, but was only man. Under this category belong the

Unitarians and Universalists, and individual false teachers in professedly Christian church-bodies, even some falsely so-called Lutheran teachers over in Germany.—This doctrine is maintained by the Lutheran Church, in the second place, against the finer errors which are rampant in all the Reformed Churches ever since the day of Zwingli. While confessing both the divinity and the humanity of Christ, they "tear the two natures in Him asunder," as Luther puts it, by teaching that, "because the Deity is incomprehensible and everywhere present, it necessarily follows that it subsists outside of its assumed humanity, and still, notwithstanding, also within it, and is personally united with it" (see *Heidelberg Catechism*, Qu. 48); and again: "We do not by any means teach that the divine nature suffered, and that Christ is still present everywhere on this earth according to His human nature" (*Second Helvetic Confession*). But what do the Scriptures say? "Ye killed *the Prince of Life*" (Acts 3:15); Christ "ascended far above all heavens, that He might fill all things" (Eph. 4:10), according to His human nature, of course; for according to His divinity He had filled all things since eternity! In the last analysis these finer Zwinglian, as well as the grosser Anti-trinitarian errors destroy the foundation of our faith. For if we cannot truthfully sing, "Oh, sorrow dread, Our God is dead," be it that a mere man died on the cross of Calvary, or that the deity was divorced from the humanity of Christ in that awful tragedy, then we are not redeemed; for only the death of the Son of God could atone for the sins of the world and satisfy the infinite justice of God.

The Son of God, then, became the Son of Man, in order to perform the great work of redemption. That is the position of the Lutheran Church as she confesses it in the Small Catechism, in Luther's matchless explanation of the Second Article of the Creed: "I believe that Jesus Christ, true God, begotten of the Father from eternity, and also true man, born of the Virgin Mary, is my Lord, who has redeemed me, a lost and condemned creature, purchased and won me from all sin, from death, and from the power of the devil." Need I cite Scripture-proof for this Lutheran position? Like a golden thread this idea of the redemptive, substitutionary character of Christ's work runs through the whole Scripture, both of the Old and the New Testament. Note only the following clear and explicit statements: "There is one God and one Mediator between God and men, the man Christ Jesus, who gave Himself a *ransom* for all" (1 Tim. 2:5, 6). "He is the *propitiation* for our sins, and not for ours only, but for the sins of the whole world" (1 John 2:2). "God sent forth His Son … made under the Law, *to redeem* them that were under the Law" (Gal. 4:4, 5). "Christ hath redeemed us from the curse of the Law, being made a curse *for us*" (Gal. 3:13). "God hath made Him to be sin *for us*, that we might be made the righteousness of God *in Him"* (2 Cor. 5:21). "We thus judge, that *if one died for all, then were all dead*; and that *He died for all*, that they which live should not henceforth live unto themselves, but unto Him which *died for them* and rose again" (2 Cor. 5:14, 15). Thus the Scriptures, in the most unequivocal and emphatic terms, teach the redemptive, substitutionary character of the work of Christ, both in His active fulfilment of the divine Law for mankind and in His passive submission to the penalty of man's sin by His suffering and death.

This Scriptural teaching concerning the work of Christ the Lutheran Church maintains over against the rationalistic vagaries of many modern "theologians," who denounce this as a "slaughter-house religion," asserting that it would have been unjust on the part of God to punish the innocent for the guilty. (In answer to this it need only to be said that even in civil law such *voluntary* substitution is considered right and is often practiced; for instance, in war men who are drafted into the army often purchase a substitute, who fights and dies in their place, and renders them forever free from liability to military service.) Rejecting this Scriptural teaching, these "theologians" have invented various other theories concerning the character and purpose of the work of Christ. One of these is the "moral influence" theory, according to which "the sole mission of Christ was to reveal the love of God in a way so moving as to melt the heart and induce men to forsake sin." Another widely accepted theory is, that Christ, both in His model life and innocent death, was the great exemplar, whom we are to follow, and by the imitation of whose example we are to work our way into heaven. Both these and other allied theories concerning the work of Christ are inadequate and unsatisfactory, because they afford the sinner neither true comfort in life nor firm hope in death. For neither one of these theories can remove the awful fact that "all have sinned and come short of the glory of God" (Rom. 3:22, 23); that, no matter how thoroughly their hearts may have been melted by the love of God as exemplified in the mission of His only Son, no matter how earnestly they may forsake the ways of sin and strive to follow their divine model, they will nevertheless remain imperfect, sinful beings, and as such under the wrath of God and excluded from heaven. No, what man needs is atonement for his sins and reconciliation with God by the blood of Christ. Nothing but the Scriptural teaching of the substitutionary, redemptive character of the work of Christ, as it is maintained by the Lutheran Church, can give the sinner a sure and firm foundation for his faith.

The Application and Appropriation of Redemption

Justification

In Christ—that is the Scriptural and the Lutheran teaching—there is complete and universal redemption. He has atoned for all the sins of every sinner. "God was in Christ, reconciling *the world* unto Himself, not imputing their trespasses unto them" (2 Cor. 5:19). "As by the offense of one" (Adam) "judgment came upon all men to condemnation, even so by the righteousness of one" (Christ) "the free gift came upon *all men* unto justification of life" (Rom. 5:18). "The blood of Jesus Christ, the Son of God, cleanses us from *all sin*" (1 John 1:7). Thus by Christ's vicarious atonement all the sins of all the human race have been blotted out, the world has been reconciled with God, in Christ God has actually justified every sinner, *i. e.,* pronounced him just and free from the guilt and penalty of sin.

But while the Lutheran Church, on the basis of Scripture, teaches the universality of Christ's redemption and the actual absolution of the world in Him, she also emphasizes, on the same basis, the necessity, on the part of the individual sinner, of accepting the salvation offered him in the Gospel. For the sinner, by rejecting Christ's salvation, can exclude himself from its benefits. "O Jerusalem, Jerusalem, you who kills the prophets, and stones those which are sent unto you, how often would I have gathered thy children together, even as a hen gathers her chickens under her wings, and *you would not!*" (Matt. 23:37.) And what is necessary on the part of the sinner to become a partaker of the great redemption? "God so loved the world that He gave His only-begotten Son, that whosoever *believeth in Him* should not perish, but have everlasting life" (John 3:16). "*Believe* on the Lord Jesus Christ, and thou shalt be saved" (Acts 16:31). Beyond this there is nothing required of the sinner in order to become a partaker of salvation and to enter heaven: no good works with which to supplement the merit of Christ, no chastisement or fasting with which to atone for unexpiated sins; no, Christ has done it all. Acceptance, by faith, of His salvation is absolutely all that is necessary on the part of the sinner.

Such is the Lutheran doctrine of justification as based on the clear teaching of Scripture. This is the great central doctrine of Christianity, which distinguishes it from all false religions, for these all teach salvation and justification by man's own works. This article the Lutheran Church alone of all the different Christian church-bodies upholds in all its Scriptural purity. In all the other churches it is obscured and vitiated to a greater or less degree. I need not dwell here on the errors of the Roman Catholic Church, which teaches directly that the sinner must earn heaven by his own good works, and pronounces its anathema upon all those who dare to affirm that he is justified by faith in Christ alone. Also in the Protestant denominations this article is seldom preached in all the Gospel purity and sweetness. It is true, exceptions are found among sectarian preachers. Some of them preach Christ crucified and salvation by faith in His blood. But the great majority are rank moralists, who tell their people to "be good" and "keep the commandments," and jumble the Law and the Gospel together by urging the sinner to fight his way through to salvation, and, instead of pointing the penitent sinner to Christ, teach him to trust in his own works, thus either driving him to despair or making a self-righteous Pharisee out of him. Over against all this work-religion the Lutheran Church unfurls the flag of the Scriptural teaching that the sinner is "justified by faith, without the deeds of the Law" (Rom. 3:28), and flings it to the winds!

Conversion

By faith in Christ the sinner becomes a partaker of His salvation. But faith is not a plant that grows in the natural heart of man. "Christ crucified is unto the Jews a stumbling-block and unto the Greeks foolishness" (1 Cor. 1:23). "The natural man receives not the things of the Spirit of God, for they are foolishness unto him; neither can he know them, because they are spiritually discerned" (1 Cor. 2:14). The natural man's understanding is "darkened"; he is "alienated from the life of God through the ignorance that is in him, because of the blindness of his heart" (Eph. 4:18). Therefore the Word of God emphasizes the necessity of a thorough change in the heart of natural man before he can become a partaker of Christ's redemption. Man must be born again to a new life (John 3:5); he must be *converted, i. e.,* "*turned* from darkness to light, and from the power of Satan unto God" (Acts 26:18); or, to express the same idea in different words: faith in Christ must be wrought in his heart; for faith is the new life in the heart of the regenerate, or converted, man. "If any man be in Christ" (by faith), "he is a new creature" (2 Cor. 5:17).

How is this change brought about? Can the sinner convert himself? Various theories have at different times been advanced within the Christian Church, ascribing to the natural man either a perfect freedom of will to decide for or against Christ (Pelagianism), or at least the power to assist in his conversion, to prepare himself for it, to cease of his own power his resistance against the operation of God's Spirit on his heart through the Gospel (Synergism). All these theories which ascribe to man any cooperation in the work of his conversion are rejected by the Lutheran Church on the basis of Scripture. "Turn Thou me, and I shall *be turned*; for Thou art the Lord, my God" (Jer. 31:18). "Turn Thou us unto Thee, O Lord, and we shall be turned" (Lam. 5:21). God must give the sinner "repentance to the acknowledging of the truth" (2 Tim. 2:25). The same almighty power of God which "commanded the light to shine out of darkness" at creation is requisite to shine into the dark heart of man in conversion, and "to give the light of the knowledge of the glory of God in the face of Jesus Christ" (2 Cor. 4:6). The same "working of His mighty power which He wrought in Christ when He raised Him from the dead" is necessary to work faith in the unconverted heart of man (Eph. 1:19, 20). Basing on these and other clear testimonies of Scripture, the Lutheran Church confesses in its Small Catechism: "I believe that I cannot by my own reason or strength believe in Jesus Christ, my Lord, or come to Him"; and the Form of Concord emphasizes that man in his conversion is "entirely passive," *i. e.*, that he cannot in the slightest degree contribute towards it, but that it is entirely and exclusively the work of the almighty power of God.

Sanctification

The necessity of sanctification is emphasized by the Lutheran Church. Not indeed as a means towards earning salvation, for we have observed before that salvation is ours entirely and alone by faith in Christ. Sanctification is not a means toward justification, but a result of it. When the sinner has been converted, *i. e.*, when he has been brought to faith in Christ and has learned to realize and appreciate the great love of God in the redemption of the lost world by His Son, then he will be moved to return that incomprehensible love, and to serve that God with all the powers of his soul in a holy life. Thus sanctification is a necessary consequence of conversion, and a life of sin is absolutely incompatible with justifying faith. This is the meaning of the Scriptural injunction to "follow holiness, without which no man shall see the Lord" (Heb. 12:14). Here, then, the Lutheran Church stands in direct contrast with the sects, which so often confound justification and sanctification, as we have already noted, teaching men to build their hope of salvation wholly or, at least, in part on their own goodness and holiness, instead of building it upon Christ alone.

Sanctification, too, is the work of God. This the Scripture plainly testifies. Thus Christ, in His sacerdotal prayer, asks the Father: "*Sanctify* them through Thy truth: Thy Word is truth" (John 17:17); and again we read: "But ye are washed, but ye are *sanctified*, but ye are justified in the name of the Lord Jesus, and *by the Spirit of our God*" (1 Cor. 6:11). Hence the Lutheran Church again confesses in the Small Catechism: "The Holy Spirit has ... sanctified me ... in the true faith." It is true, there is a difference between the natural, unconverted man, who is "dead in trespasses and sins," and the regenerate, converted man, in whom a new spiritual life has been enkindled. The former, as we have seen, is totally unable to contribute towards his conversion, while the latter can and does assist in, and cooperate towards, his sanctification. But still we must not liken this cooperation of the regenerate man and the Holy Spirit in sanctification to two horses pulling the same wagon. No; God's Spirit must always remain the impelling power; He must sustain the spiritual life and nourish the spiritual powers in the Christian, which enable him to "follow after holiness," and to assist in his sanctification. Also in this the Lutheran Church differs from the other Protestant Churches, which often talk about sanctification as though it were entirely man's work, and urge the Christian on towards a holier and better life in terms that would lead him to believe that the power to overcome sin and to live right lies entirely within himself.

Sanctification consists in striving to live according to the will of God, or, to express it differently, in performing such works as God has commanded. For only those are good and holy works which God has commanded. "In vain do they worship Me, teaching for doctrines the commandments of men" (Matt. 15:9). Obedience to human ordinances, adding to, or contravening, the Word of God, is not serving God and is not conducive toward advancing us in sanctification.

Here again is an important point of difference between the Lutheran Church and other Churches. To the latter the word of Christ quoted in the preceding paragraph applies in a greater or less degree; they all, in some measure, "teach for doctrines the commandments of men." The worst offender in this direction is again the Roman Catholic Church, with its boasted holiness of monastic celibacy, its rosaries, its fast-days, etc. But also in the Protestant denominations there is much of this leaven of man-invented ordinances, *e. g.*, their legalistic Sabbath idea, their temperance fanaticism, etc. Here, too, the Lutheran Church stands squarely upon the Word of God, teaching no other works as necessary for sanctification than those commanded by God.

Sanctification can never become complete and perfect in this life. This is another proposition maintained by the Lutheran Church on the basis of Scripture. "If we say that we have no sin, we deceive ourselves, and the truth is not in us" (1 John 1:8). "Who can say, I have made my heart clean, I am pure from my sin?" (Prov. 20:9.) "There is not a just man upon earth that doeth good and sins not" (Eccl. 7:21). Even the great Apostle Paul was constrained to confess of himself: "Not as though I had already attained, either were already perfect" (Phil. 3:12).

Here, then, is another distinct line of cleavage between the Lutheran, Scriptural position and that of several other Protestant Churches, notably the Methodists and the so-called "Holiness" churches, which maintain that a Christian already in this life may attain to perfection in holiness. This is a very dangerous error, because if a man has once formed the idea that he is perfect, he is very much inclined to regard himself a fit subject for heaven by virtue of his own holiness, and therefore to despise the Savior and His atonement for sin.

ELECTION, OR PREDESTINATION

The Lutheran view, as based on the Scriptures and expressed especially in the Formula of

Concord, is this, that in eternity, according to the good pleasure of His will, in Christ, God elected all those who will finally be saved to eternal salvation, and that this decree of predestination includes everything necessary for their salvation, to wit, their conversion in time and their preservation in faith until death, thus making it impossible for the elect to be lost. Formula of Concord: "The eternal election of God not only foresees and foreknows the salvation of the elect, but through His gracious will and good pleasure in Christ Jesus is also a cause which procures, works, facilitates, and promotes our salvation and whatever pertains thereto; upon it also our salvation is so founded that 'the gates of hell cannot prevail against it' (Matt. 16:18). 'Neither shall any man pluck My sheep out of My hand' (John 10:28)."—On the other hand, God did not elect or predestinate any man or number of men to damnation. Also those who are lost have been redeemed by Christ, and God earnestly desires their salvation, and offers them salvation in the Gospel. "They deny the Lord that bought them, and bring upon themselves swift destruction" (2 Pet. 2:1). "God will have all men to be saved and to come unto the knowledge of the truth" (1 Tim. 2:4).—Now, this leaves an unsolved mystery for our reason: If God earnestly desires the salvation of all sinners, and all sinners, as we learned under the article of conversion, are alike "dead in trespasses and sins," then why is it that not all are saved? This mystery the Lutheran Church does not try to solve, because God's Word leaves it unsolved, placing alongside of each other, without any attempt at harmonizing them to reason, these two truths, that those who are saved, are saved solely through the grace of God, while those who are lost, are lost through their own fault. "O Israel, you have destroyed yourself; but in Me is your help" (Hos. 13:9).

The Lutheran Church holds this position, in the first place, over against the Calvinists, who seek to solve the mystery by placing the cause for both, the salvation of some and the damnation of others, in God, by teaching a double absolute decree of predestination, *viz.*, that God not only predestinated some to eternal life, but that He also predestinated the others to eternal damnation; that He therefore excluded these from all possibility of salvation in that He neither sent His Son to redeem them, nor calls them seriously and effectually by the Gospel.—In the second place, the Lutheran Church also maintains this doctrine of election over against Synergism, *i.e.*, the doctrine which tries to solve the mystery by placing a difference in the conduct of man towards the Gospel, affirming that the greater number are lost because of their obstinate resistance to God's Spirit, and the rest are saved because they yield more readily to the influences of the Spirit, and thus, in a way, contribute to, and cooperate in, their conversion. Both these theories are rationalistic in tendency, that is, they seek to make the doctrine of predestination palatable to human reason, in direct contravention of the plain teaching of Scripture.

THE MEANS OF GRACE

Our salvation is by grace. It was God's grace and mercy that moved Him to redeem fallen and lost mankind through the merits and death of His Son, and it is His grace that now moves Him to offer and convey this salvation to the individual sinner. "By grace are ye saved, through faith; and that not of yourselves: it is the gift of God; not of works, lest any man should boast" (Eph. 2:8, 9). "Grace first contrived the way to save rebellious man; And all the steps that grace display Which drew the wondrous plan." And the means through which God conveys this gracious salvation to man are what is meant by the title at the head of this section, "the Means of Grace." Or perhaps I ought to put it thus: That is what the Lutheran Church understands by the term, in distinction from other Churches, notably the Methodist Churches, which comprise under the term rather the means by which man appropriates to himself the grace of God.—According to the Lutheran view these "means of grace" comprise the Word of God and the Sacraments.

The Word of God

Just a word about this term. By the "Word of God" Lutherans mean the whole Bible, which they accept in its entirety as the inspired word of God, according to its own testimony: "All Scripture is given by inspiration of God" (2 Tim. 3:16), and many other passages (compare, *e. g.*, 2 Pet. 1:19–21; 1 Cor. 2:13; Acts 1:16; 3:18, etc.).—This conception of the Bible as the inspired word of God the Lutheran Church maintains and emphasizes over against the modern theories of the so-called Higher Critics, who would make out the Bible to be a merely human or, at best, a divine-human book, claiming for themselves the right to determine what is divine and what is human in it, whose vagaries are eating like a canker into the very vitals of Christianity.

The maintenance of this truth, that the Bible is the inspired Word of God, is of the utmost importance for a double reason. In the first place, only then does the Bible furnish us a firm basis of belief and faith, if it is in its entirety the Word of God, for only then is it infallible and authoritative in matters of faith. In the second place, only its divine character can constitute it a means of grace, *i. e.*, as stated above, a means of conveying grace to the sinner, for only in the living Word of God, whether in its written or preached form, can there be inherent the power of bringing divine grace to the sinner and of giving him the power to accept it. That this power is possessed by the Word is plainly taught in it: "I am not ashamed of the Gospel of Jesus Christ; for it is the power of God unto salvation to everyone that believes" (Rom. 1:16). "So then, faith cometh by hearing, and hearing by the Word of God" (Rom. 10:17). "That from a child thou hast known the Holy Scriptures, which are able to make thee wise unto salvation through faith which is in Christ Jesus" (2 Tim. 3:15).

The Sacraments

The word "Sacrament" is not a Biblical, but an ecclesiastical term. Our Church defines it as "a sacred act, ordained by God, wherein He by certain external means connected with His Word, offers, conveys, and seals unto men the grace which Christ has merited." According to this definition three things are required to constitute a Sacrament: 1) God's institution, 2) an earthly, visible element, or elements, 3) the impartation of divine grace.—The Lutheran Church, then, does not look upon the Sacraments as "mere outward signs of an inward grace," but in conformity with Scripture holds them to be real "means of grace," *i.e.*, actual means through which the Holy Spirit works and preserves and strengthens faith, and conveys and seals divine grace to the sinner.

The above definition also limits the number of Sacraments to two, Baptism and the Lord's Supper, for only these two contain all the three requisite elements. It is well known that the Catholic Church numbers seven sacraments, adding to those mentioned the following: penitence, confirmation, matrimony, holy orders, extreme unction. But all of these lack one or more of the three elements that constitute a Sacrament; *e.g.*, matrimony was instituted by God, but is merely a civil matter and conveys no divine grace; confirmation lacks the divine institution and is only an ecclesiastical rite, etc. But while the term "Sacrament," as was stated above, is not of Biblical origin, and we cannot, therefore, accuse another church of false doctrine for differing with us on the definition and number of the Sacraments, yet we would certainly not be willing to depart from our position on this subject, because these two ordinances, Baptism and the Lord's Supper, occupy a unique position in God's economy of grace and should therefore not be thrown together with other ordinances, whether of divine or human origin, which fall into an altogether different category.—After these introductory remarks on the subject of the Sacraments in general, we now proceed to a consideration of the Lutheran position with regard to the individual Sacraments.

Baptism

Three phases of this subject must occupy us, in which the Lutheran position differs from that of other churches. In the first place *the efficacy* of the Sacrament. As stated already in the introductory remarks, the Lutheran Church teaches that the Sacraments are not only outward signs or emblems, but actual conveyors, of divine grace. Accordingly, she also teaches that Baptism "works forgiveness of sins, delivers from death and the devil, and gives eternal salvation to all who believe this." This is Scriptural doctrine. Baptism works regeneration or the new birth. Paul calls it "the washing of regeneration and renewing of the Holy Spirit" (Titus 3:5), and Christ Himself says that man must "be born of the water and the Spirit" in order to enter into the kingdom of heaven. Baptism, then, works the new life of faith, by which a man becomes a partaker of Christ's merits and receives the forgiveness of sins: "Ye are all the children of God by faith in Christ Jesus. For as many of you as have been baptized into Christ have put on Christ" (Gal. 3:26, 27). Thus, then, does Baptism work forgiveness of sins. "Repent, and be baptized, every one of you, in the name of Jesus Christ *for the remission of sins*" (Acts 2:38). "Be baptized, and *wash away thy sins*" (Acts 22:16). And thus Baptism delivers us also from death and the devil, for it is through sin that these enemies have power over us, so that a baptized Christian can triumph with St. Paul: "O death, where is thy sting? O grave, where is thy victory? The sting of death is sin; and the strength of sin is the Law. But thanks be to God, which giveth us the victory through our Lord Jesus Christ" (1 Cor. 15:55–57). And thus Baptism also confers eternal salvation. "He that believeth and is baptized *shall be saved*" (Mark 16:16). "Baptism doth also now *save us*" (1 Pet. 3:21).—These passages surely teach as plainly and unequivocally as human language can teach that Baptism is not, as the Reformed Churches claim, merely an emblem, a type, of regeneration and the washing away of sins, but that it actually effects and accomplishes these great things.

Another important point of controversy with regard to Baptism is the question: *Who is to be baptized*? The Lutheran Church, in common with a number of the other Christian Churches, maintains that Baptism is intended for all, adults and children, also for children of the most tender age, while the Baptist churches maintain that it is to be administered to adults only. The main ground upon which the latter base this contention is that small children cannot have conscious faith, cannot know and understand the purpose of Baptism, and therefore can receive no benefit from it.—Over against this view we teach, upon the basis of Scripture, 1) that also little children can have faith, according to Christ's own words: "Whoso shall offend one of these little ones which believe in Me" (Matt. 18:6). "Verily I say unto you, Whosoever shall not receive the kingdom of God as a little child, he shall not enter therein" (Mark 10:16); 2) that little children stand in need of Baptism, because they are "flesh born of flesh" and therefore must be "born again of the water and of the Spirit" (John 3:5, 6); 3) that the commission to "baptize all *nations"* (Matt. 28:19) comprises children as well as adults; 4) that infant baptism was evidently practiced by the apostles, who baptized entire families (*e. g.*, the jailer's family at Philippi, Acts 16:33; Lydia's, Acts 16:15), which normally consist of parents and children; 5) that, by analogy with the Old Testament, baptism ought to be administered to infants as well as its prototype, circumcision (Col. 2:11, 12); that as Jewish male children were admitted into God's covenant by the rite of circumcision on their eighth day, so children are now to be admitted into the New Testament covenant by Baptism in their early infancy.

The third important matter with reference to the subject of Baptism, and the second question at issue between Baptists on the one hand and the Lutheran and other Protestant Churches on the other, is *the mode of baptism, i. e.,* the question how the water in Baptism is to be applied. The former maintain that Baptism must be administered by immersion and that no other mode is admissible, while the latter claim that any mode of applying the water, whether by immersion or pouring or sprinkling, is valid. The argument of Baptists for their position is simply this, that the Greek word "baptize," both in the Bible and in Greek profane literature, always means to immerse or dip under water, and they have gone so far as to get out a special version of the Bible, in which they substitute "immerse" for "baptize" in all the passages in which the word occurs. The opponents of this theory, prominent among these we Lutherans, assert, on the contrary, that "baptize" means not only to immerse, but denotes any kind of washing in the New Testament. Thus in Mark 7:3 we read of diverse kinds of washings, such as of pots, brazen vessels, and tables, which the Jews observed. The word in the original, which is here rendered by "washing," is "baptisms,"—baptisms of cups, etc.,—and it is evident at first glance that this term here does not mean washing by immersion only, but any kind of washing.—In Matt. 3:11 John the Baptist says of Christ; "He shall baptize you with the Holy Spirit and with fire," and Acts 2:16 the Apostle Peter explains this phrase "*baptize* with the Holy Spirit" by a reference to the prophecy of Joel: "And it shall come to pass in the last days, I will *pour out* My Spirit upon all flesh." Here, then, we have baptism by pouring! The subject is too extensive to permit us to enter into a detailed discussion of it here. We believe these few passages are sufficient to overthrow the Baptist argument.

The Lord's Supper

In the doctrine concerning the Lord's Supper there are especially two points of difference between the Lutheran and other Churches, which it will be necessary for us to consider. There is first the question of the true presence of Christ's body and blood in the Sacrament. In regard to this question three different views are held in different Churches. The Reformed denominations, following the rationalistic leading of Zwingli, all deny the true presence, and affirm that bread and wine are mere symbols or representations, but not real conveyors, of Christ's body and blood. This is a rationalistic view, I said, because it is mainly from arguments of reason that the true presence is rejected: it is considered unreasonable that Christ's body and blood should really be received by the communicant with his mouth in, with, and under the bread and wine.—That is the one extreme. The other is the Roman Catholic view of transubstantiation, *i.e.*, the doctrine that in the Sacrament the substance of bread and wine is changed into the substance of the body and blood of Christ by virtue of the consecration of the priest, and that nothing but the outward form and attributes of the former remains. (Closely linked with this error, and directly flowing from it, is the other, that bread, once consecrated, remains the body of Christ, also after the administration of the Sacrament, and its consequent abuse for adoration [Corpus Christi Day] and for "unbloody sacrifice" in the Mass. From it also flows the abuse of distributing the Sacrament to the laity under one kind; for the reason assigned for this mutilation of the Sacrament is, that the body always contains the blood, and that there is no need, therefore, of drinking the latter separately in the wine.)

Over against these two extremes the Lutheran Church teaches that the true, natural body and blood of Christ are actually present and received by every communicant with the mouth of his body together with the consecrated bread and wine. We deny, then, on the one hand, that nothing but bread and wine is received as the Reformed teach, and on the other hand, that only body and blood of Christ are received, as the Romanists assert.—Here it will be necessary, however, to define our position with reference to some terms that are persistently applied to our doctrine by men in other churches, and which, like Banquo's ghost, will not down in spite of persistent denial on our part. The Lutheran Church, then, is credited with teaching "impanation," *i.e.*, the inclusion of Christ's body and blood in the bread and wine; we are also represented as teaching "consubstantiation," *i.e.*, the mingling of Christ's body and blood with the substance of the bread and wine. Lutherans reject these terms applied to their teaching by others, because they would imply that the heavenly elements are received in a natural or carnal manner, just as the earthly elements, an imputation which we emphatically repel. For the Lutheran position is, that, while Christ's body and blood are really and truly present in the Sacrament and received by the mouth, yet this is not a natural, but a supernatural, heavenly, or to use the technical term, a sacramental eating and drinking.

Also here the Lutheran Church stands on Scriptural ground. It accepts Christ's words: "This is My body, which is given for you"; "This is My blood of the New Testament, which is shed for you," in their natural, literal meaning, while the Reformed denominations, as is well known, give a figurative, typical meaning to them, explaining them as meaning: "This represents, typifies, My body and blood," etc. Lutherans insist that the words must be taken in a literal sense, because they are the words of a divine covenant and testament, which we have no right to interpret according to our own ideas. "Though it be but a man's covenant (or testament), yet, if it be confirmed, no man disannuls or adds to it" (Gal. 3:15). Even a man's testament or will is accepted just as it reads; much more ought we to accept the last testament of our divine Lord and Savior without putting our own construction upon it.— Another important proof for the real presence is 1 Cor. 11:27, 29. "Whosoever shall eat this bread, and drink this cup of the Lord, unworthily, shall be *guilty of the body and blood of the Lord.*—He that eats and drinks unworthily, eats and drinks damnation to himself, *not discerning the Lord's body.*" If the unworthy communicant becomes guilty, not of the emblems, but of the body and blood of the Lord itself; and if he eats and drinks damnation to himself by failing to discern the Lord's body, *i.e.*, if he commits a grievous sin against Christ's body, then this must be present and be received also by the unworthy communicant.

Closely allied with the foregoing subject is that of the efficacy of the Sacrament. It is natural for the Reformed Churches, which believe that bread and wine are merely emblems of an absent Christ, to see in the Sacrament nothing but a commemorative meal, designed merely to remind us of the suffering and death of our Redeemer, but without special power or efficacy to confer spiritual blessings. And it is just as easy for the Roman Catholic Church, with its doctrine of transubstantiation, to arrive at its doctrine of the *opus operatum, i.e.,* that the mere act of going to the Sacrament constitutes a good deed, by which man merits favor in the sight of God.—In distinction also from these two extremes the Lutheran Church again teaches that "in the Sacrament forgiveness of sin, life, and salvation are given us through these words, 'Given and shed for you for the remission of sins.' " To express it differently: Christ gives to each communicant His body and blood as a token and pledge that this body was given into death *for him*, and that His blood was shed for the remission of *his* sins, in order thus to strengthen and preserve his faith, to assure him personally, individually, of the forgiveness of sins and the certainty of his salvation.

Summary of the Lutheran position on the Means of Grace.—The other Protestant Churches think and speak lightly of the means of grace, as we have had occasion to notice in the preceding pages. They deny to the Sacraments any power to work and preserve faith and to confer grace and salvation, and they teach that the Spirit of God works independently of the Word and the Sacraments on the hearts of men. Moreover some of them lay great stress upon the efforts of man, by prayer, penitence, and struggling to draw the Spirit of God down into his heart, and they number these things among the means of grace. The Lutheran Church, on the other hand, teaches and confesses that the Gospel, *i. e.*, the Word and the Sacraments, are the only means by which God's Spirit ordinarily performs His work in the hearts of men, by which He calls them to Christ, converts them, sanctifies them, and keeps them in the faith. "So, then, faith cometh by hearing, and hearing by the Word of God" (Rom. 10:17). "The Gospel of Jesus Christ is the power of God unto salvation" (Rom. 1:16). "By one Spirit are we all baptized into one body, ... and have been all made to drink into one Spirit" (1 Cor. 12:13).

The Ministry

Closely allied to the subject of the Means of Grace, which we have just now considered, is that of the ministry of the Word. In the same connection in which the Apostle Paul says that "faith cometh by hearing, and hearing by the Word of God," he also says: "How shall they believe in Him of whom they have not heard? and how shall they hear without a preacher?" (Rom. 10:14.) For although also in its written form "the Gospel of Jesus Christ is the power of God unto salvation," although also the Holy Scriptures, the written Word of God, "are able to make us wise unto salvation through faith which is in Christ Jesus" (2

Tim. 3:15), yet, in order to spread the glad tidings of salvation, it was necessary that it should be publicly proclaimed, and for this reason God has made it the duty of every Christian to confess Christ, but in addition has instituted a special ministry, and sends out His messengers into the world to carry the Gospel-call, "Come, for all things are now ready," to every nation, and kindred, and tongue, and people.

The ministry, then, is an institution of God. "How shall they preach, except they be sent?" (Rom. 10:15.) "Go ye into all the world and preach the Gospel to every creature" (Mark 16:15). "Go ye and teach all nations, baptizing them, ... teaching them to observe all things whatsoever I have commanded you" (Matt. 28:19). Christ "gave some, apostles; and some, prophets; and some, evangelists; and some, pastors and teachers, for the perfecting of the saints, for the work of the ministry, for the edifying of the body of Christ" (Eph. 4:11, 12; compare 1 Cor. 12:28). Hence Luther, in the Small Catechism, rightly speaks of pastors as "the called ministers of Christ." They are not servants of men, but of Christ, although called through the instrumentality of men; and they are "called ministers," not hired under a contract, like ordinary laborers. Thus the Lutheran Church teaches and believes that the ministry is of divine appointment, that the incumbents of the office are divinely called, and that God also calls them to their various positions and removes them from one field to another, albeit through the instrumentality of the congregations. Also in this, then, she distinguishes herself from other Churches, which countenance and practice the hiring of preachers by the year, and moving them about by their bishops at stated intervals. And so she also rejects the view, so prevalent nowadays, which looks upon the ministry as being on a level with other, merely secular occupations, as a mere means of gaining a livelihood, which view is largely responsible for the degrading of the holy office by many of its incumbents in other churches through their worldly-mindedness, sensationalism in the pulpit, and lecturing on politics, questions of the day, etc., instead of preaching the Gospel according to Christ's injunction.

Because the ministry is God's institution, therefore we Lutherans, as Luther's Small Catechism puts it, "believe that when the called ministers of Christ deal with us by His divine command, ... this is as valid and certain, in heaven also, as if Christ, our dear Lord, dealt with us Himself." In other words, in the ministrations of their sacred office pastors act in the place of Christ, as God's mouthpieces. Christ, God, preaches, reproves, teaches, comforts, baptizes through them. It is this that gives to their preaching and administration of the Sacraments the power to convert sinners, to work and preserve faith in their hearts. The Word of God, also when preached by weak, sinful men, is always endowed with divine power; the Gospel of Jesus Christ, also when preached by men, "is the power of God unto salvation."

In this connection a special function of the ministry still needs to be considered, *viz.*, the power of absolution, or announcing the forgiveness of sins to repentant sinners. Also of this Luther says in the Catechism that we should "receive absolution, or forgiveness, from the confessor"—*i.e.*, the pastor—"as from God Himself, and in no wise doubt, but firmly believe, that by it our sins are forgiven before God in heaven." This Lutheran position is particularly offensive to the Reformed denominations, because, as they say, it gives to a man the power to forgive sins, and, "Who can forgive sins but God only?" But when we bear in mind what was said above, that in all the pastor does, as pastor, he acts in the stead and by the command of Christ, as His "ambassador" (2 Cor. 5:20), also this function of the ministerial office becomes readily understandable. Indeed, Paul applies the above principle to this very function of the office when he writes: "If I forgave anything, to whom I forgave it, for your sakes forgave I it *in the person of Christ*" (2 Cor. 2:10). So it is not the minister, in reality, that pronounces the absolution, but Christ does it through him. And just as the business transacted by the representative of a king or other ruler at a foreign capital in the ruler's name has the same validity as though it were transacted by the ruler in person, so also the forgiveness pronounced by the "ambassador" of Christ "is as valid and certain, in heaven also, as if Christ, our dear Lord, dealt with us Himself."

SUNDAY

The public use of the means of grace—the proclamation of the Gospel and the administration of the Sacraments—is the means by which the kingdom of God is built and extended. But for the effective accomplishment of this purpose it is necessary to have a specified place and time, so that people may know where and when to assemble to hear the preaching of the Word. Hence the Christian Church has always observed a special day—Sunday—on which to assemble for public worship. And since there is a divergence of views on this subject on the part of the Lutheran Church and other Churches, we will discuss the matter here for want of a better place.

The Lutheran position with regard to Sunday is this, that this day is not the successor of the Old Testament Sabbath, that is to say, that it has not been put in the place of that day by divine command, but that it is a human, an ecclesiastical ordinance, established merely for the sake of convenience; that the Sabbath belonged to the types and shadows of the Old Dispensation, and therefore automatically came to an end when the body or reality appeared in Christ; that in the New Testament no particular day of the week, in fact, no day at all, is divinely ordained as a day of rest and worship, but that the choice and observance of such a day belongs to the matters left to our Christian liberty; and that Sunday, the first day of the week, was chosen by the Apostolic Church, in the exercise of this liberty, for the purpose of showing that the Sabbath-command is no more binding upon us, and for the reason that Christ arose from the dead on this day. Scriptural proof for the correctness of this view: "Upon the first day of the week, when the disciples came together to break bread" (celebrate Communion), "Paul preached unto them" (Acts 20:7). "Upon the first day of the week let every one of you lay by him in store as God hath prospered him" (1 Cor. 16:2). "One man esteems one day above another; another esteems every day alike. Let every man be fully persuaded in his own mind. He that regards the day regards it unto the Lord; and he that regards not the day, to the Lord he doth not regard it." (Rom. 14:5, 6. If God had commanded the observance of Sunday, certainly no one could serve the Lord by disregarding this day!) "Let no man judge you in meat, or in drink, or in respect of an holy-day, or of the new moon, or of the Sabbath-days: which are a shadow of things to come; but the body is of Christ" (Col. 2:16, 17).

Opposing views: 1) Of the Reformed Churches, that Sunday is the New Testament Sabbath, of divine obligation; 2) of the Catholic Church, that Sunday was ordained and imposed by the infallible Church, and is therefore obligatory upon its members; 3) of the Sabbatarian sects (Seventh-day Adventists and others), that the Old Testament Sabbath-law is still in force, and that Christians, therefore, are under obligation to observe the seventh day of the week instead of the first.

THE LAST JUDGMENT

The Lutheran Church believes and teaches that our Lord Jesus Christ will, at the end of the world, appear for the second time to raise the dead, to destroy this world, to judge the quick and the dead, and to assign to each man his eternal doom "according to that he hath done in the body, whether it be good or bad." See Christ's description of the great judgment, Matt. 25; also 2 Pet. 3, and many other passages of the New Testament. The time of the Judgment is not known to us. "Of that day and that hour knows no man, no, not the angels which are in heaven, neither the Son, but the Father." (Mark 13:32. Even the Son, in His state of humiliation and as to His human nature, had laid aside, together with the use of His divine omniscience, the knowledge of the time appointed for the Judgment. Compare also the following verses of the chapter.) "As the lightning comes out of the east, and shines even unto the west, so shall also the coming of the Son of Man be" (Matt. 24:27). "The day of the Lord will come as a thief in the night" (2 Pet. 3:10).

Indeed, certain signs precede and herald the approach of the Judgment (compare Matt. 24; 2 Thess. 2:1–12; 2 Pet. 3:3, 4); and since these signs predicted in Scripture have in large measure been fulfilled, or are now in process of fulfilment, we may be certain that the great day of the Lord is close at hand. But no man can know how close, for "one day with the Lord is as a thousand years and a thousand years as one day" (2 Pet. 3:8). Hence the Lutheran Church has always rejected the fantastical dreams of certain would-be prophets, such as the Rev. Miller and Mrs. White, of the Seventh-day Adventists, and others who have presumed to predict the exact date of the end of the world.—The Lutheran Church also rejects the belief in

The Millennium

that is, the belief that prior to the final Judgment Christ will come again in visible form to raise the saints, and to reign with them a thousand years upon earth, while Satan shall be bound and restrained from tempting and vexing the Church. This doctrine is held by many Christians in different denominations, is proclaimed especially by the adherents of the notorious Russell and by the Seventh-day Adventists, and has been espoused even by some Lutherans. It is derived, by a false literal interpretation, from the 20th chapter of Revelation.

We cannot here attempt a full discussion of this prophetic passage. Suffice it to say that this is a passage in a prophetic book which speaks much in figurative and typical language, much of which is dark and unintelligible until made clear by fulfilment. Also in this passage we dare not press the literal sense of the words, and perhaps no certain and authentic explanation of it will ever be possible this side the light of glory. But all attempted explanations must conform to the rule of Biblical interpretation, that they dare not militate against the plain sense of other clear passages of Scripture. Now the New Testament plainly teaches: 1) that Christ at His second advent will come, not for a visible reign upon earth, but for judgment, and to bring eternal salvation to His Christians. "Christ was once offered to bear the sins of many; and unto them that look for Him shall He appear *the second time* without sin, *unto salvation*" (Heb. 9:28); 2) that the kingdom of Christ upon earth is a spiritual, not visible kingdom, subject to hardship and persecution, until the end of the world. My kingdom is not of this world" (John 18:36). "We must through much tribulation enter into the kingdom of God" (Acts 14:22). And just during the last time preceding the Judgment, tribulations and hardships are to be more severe than ever before. See Matt. 24 and 2 Pet. 3, quoted above. Hence all vagaries which would make us expect such a temporal reign of Christ and His saints on earth for a thousand years must be rejected.

ETERNAL PUNISHMENT OF THE WICKED

The question whether the wicked will be punished in all eternity is largely answered in the negative. Not only are there whole church-bodies that so answer it, but also many members of other churches no longer believe in such a punishment. The Universalists, *e. g.*, maintain that, while there will be a punishment of the wicked in the next world, that punishment will be corrective rather than punitive, that the wicked will be made better by it, and so all finally will enter heaven after being purified from their sins. They believe in a universal salvation of all mankind, whence their name.—The Seventh-day Adventists deny the existence of hell and of a punishment after death altogether, and teach the annihilation, or destruction, of the wicked.

What do the Scriptures say? Let us hear only a few expressions of our Lord Himself: "Depart from Me, ye cursed, into everlasting fire, prepared for the devil and his angels…. And these shall go away into everlasting punishment" (Matt. 25:41, 46). And in His warning against offenses He says: "It is better for thee to enter into life halt or maimed, rather than, having two hands or two feet, to be cast into everlasting fire. It is better for thee to enter into life with one eye, rather than, having two eyes, to be cast into hell-fire" (Matt. 18:8, 9).— Passages like these could be multiplied from the New Testament. And the Lutheran Church strictly adheres to God's Word also in this question, although aware that in so doing she flies in the face of modern sentiment.

Is there a personal devil? This is another question that is largely answered in the negative. The devil knows, if he can get people to believe that there is neither devil nor hell, he can the more easily seduce them into sin, and so lure them into his snares. But also with regard to this question the Bible speaks in no uncertain terms. Christ Himself was tempted by the devil (Matt. 4:3–11). And we are repeatedly warned to beware of his temptations: "Put on the whole armor of God, that ye may be able to stand against the wiles of the devil" (Eph. 6:11). "Be sober, be vigilant, because your adversary, the devil, as a roaring lion, walks about, seeking whom he may devour" (1 Pet. 5:8). These passages, too, might be multiplied, but those we have given are so plain that they need no further corroboration. The Lutheran Church stands on firm Scriptural ground when, in opposition to modern sentiment, she maintains the existence of a personal devil.

PART II

Confessions of the Lutheran Church

The Lutheran Church lays great stress upon the purity of doctrine. Therefore the subject of doctrine forms the first part of this book and occupies the largest space in it. In formulating her doctrines and fortifying them against attack, the Lutheran Church ever and anon appeals to the Scriptures. These are the sole source of her teaching. And the reader cannot but have noticed that also in the preceding pages of this treatise all doctrines are proved from this source alone. But in defining and defending her doctrinal position over against error, she early drew up and adopted certain writings, known as Creeds or Confessions, by which she desires to be judged and distinguished from other Churches. These Confessions, then, are not a source of doctrine, but only a definition of it. Lutherans do not place them on a level with the Scriptures, but subordinate them to these. They are not, as some opponents have termed them, a "paper pope," designed to tyrannize over the consciences of Lutherans—for our conscience can be bound by the Word of God alone. As the dogmaticians express it: The Scripture alone is the *norma normans*, the regulating norm of our faith; the Confessions are the *norma normata*, the secondary norm, drawn from, and formulated according to, the Word of God. Or to put it still differently: If one would know what is correct Christian doctrine, the Lutheran will point him to the Bible; but if he asks what is the Lutheran doctrine on any given question, then he refers him to the Confessions, because these show how the Lutheran Church understands and interprets the Bible. Hence Lutheran bodies, congregations as well as synods, commonly define their doctrinal standpoint in their constitutions in these or similar words: "We confess the canonical books of the Old and New Testaments to be the inspired Word of God, and therefore the only rule of faith and life, and the confessional writings of the Evangelical Lutheran Church to be a correct presentation of the doctrines of this Word."

Every member of the Lutheran Church is therefore expected, and rightly so, to subscribe not only to the Bible, but also to the Confessions. If he cannot consistently do so, he is not a Lutheran, hence cannot truthfully become or remain a member of a church whose doctrines he condemns. Nor can the Lutheran Church tolerate such members, because from the Bible she is convinced that in every point in which they deviate from the Lutheran Confessions they reject the plain Word of God. (This is not saying that such a person cannot be a Christian; for a Christian may err, and not all Christians are in the Lutheran Church. But while he may be a Christian, yet his place certainly is not in the pale of that Church as long as he disagrees with her doctrinal position as laid down in her Confessions.) And of course, what has just been said of every member of the Church applies in a still higher degree to the public teachers of the Church. Lutheran pastors and theological professors are asked by their congregations and synods for an unequivocal subscription to the Lutheran Confessions and a faithful adherence to the doctrinal position there defined.

Much has been said and written against this confessional attitude of the Lutheran Church. The spirit of ecclesiastical unionism and doctrinal indifference that is rampant in our days, particularly also in our country, where the complete separation of Church and State and the unrestricted religious liberty fosters the multiplication of sects and churches, naturally opposes any such determined confessionalism as is practiced by the Lutheran Church. Sentiments such as these commonly prevail: One church is as good as another, one has about as much truth as another, and it is arrogance for one church to maintain that it is in possession of all the truth. The differences that separate the various church-bodies are of minor importance and ought not to be emphasized, and there is no need of creeds and confessions which can serve only this purpose. Rather let us forget our differences and emphasize our agreements and strive for a union of at least all the Protestant Churches. Therefore let us cast overboard our creeds and confessions that separate us. "Back to Christ! Back to the Bible!" let that be our slogan.—Now, this slogan sounds very specious. But when we sift it down, we generally find that it means just the opposite, that, instead of trying to get back to Christ and the Bible, these people are, as a rule, moving farther and farther away from both; that the "Christianity" which they profess is mostly a shallow morality, a shell without the kernel, a "Christianity" with the real Christ left out. Lutheran confessionalism, however, being an unswerving adherence to divine truth, is at the same time adherence to Christ and to His Word. In the midst of the chaos of multiplying churches with their false unionism the Lutheran Church is not in need of the slogan: Back to Christ and the Bible! Why? Because with her glorious Confessions she is, as she always has been, standing four-square upon this rock of our Christian faith.

ECUMENICAL SYMBOLS

The Lutheran Confessions, an enumeration and brief description of which will naturally be looked for in this connection, are contained in the Book of Concord, published 1580. In their order of succession they are the following: The three so-called Ecumenical Symbols: the Apostles', Nicene, and Athanasian Creeds; the Augsburg Confession and the Apology of the same; the Smalcald Articles; the Small and the Large Catechism of Luther; the Formula of Concord. Of these nine confessions the first three, the Ecumenical Symbols, have come down to the Lutheran Church from the early centuries of the Christian era, and she has adopted them as her own, because they express, in a forcible and admirable manner, the fundamental truths of the Christian religion. They are called "ecumenical symbols" because the truths which they contain are believed and confessed by all Christians of all ages and of all places.

The first of these is the *Apostles' Creed.* According to the belief which was current during the medieval ages, this symbol was framed by the apostles in Jerusalem before starting on their missionary journey, each apostle contributing a sentence. This theory, however, was doubted ever since and even before the Reformation, and disproved by modern researches. Though containing phrases and statements which were in use in the apostolic age and existing in a briefer form before A. D. 150, the Apostles' Creed in its present form was not complete before the end of the fifth century. It was the result of a slow growth which had its origin in the formula of baptism and the baptismal confession, 1 Tim. 6:12. From time to time additions and changes were made, as the springing up of heresies made it necessary to unfold the apostolic truth, until its present form was arrived at. But although its apostolic origin has been disproved, the Apostles' Creed nevertheless rightfully bears its name, for it certainly does contain a pithy and concise summary of the doctrine of the apostles as contained in the New Testament. And it is in this sense that the Lutheran Church has embodied the Apostles' Creed in its confessional writings.— Perhaps a slight verbal change should be noted, which Luther made in the second point of the

Third Article, where the word "Christian" is substituted for "catholic" in the phrase "The holy catholic Church," because the Roman Catholic Church had arrogated to itself this latter term.

The second of the three General Creeds is the *Nicene Creed*, so named from the Council of Nicaea, in Asia Minor, held in the year 325, and attended by 318 bishops. It was also originally a baptismal formula, which had been in vogue before, and was adopted by the council, with a number of changes and additions, as an ecclesiastical symbol against the Arian heresy, which denied that Christ was true God, coequal and consubstantial with the Father. The Nicene Creed received its present form from the second Ecumenical Council, held 381 at Constantinople and attended by 150 bishops. The last addition, made as late as 589 by the council at Toledo, was the phrase "and from the Son" in the statement concerning the Holy Spirit: "Who proceeds from the Father and the Son," which, however, the Greek Church refused to accept, and which, later, contributed in bringing about its separation from the Western Church. The Nicene Creed is still valuable as a powerful testimony to the true deity of Christ and the Holy Trinity over against modern assailants of that fundamental Christian doctrine.

The same applies to the third of the ecumenical symbols, the *Athanasian Creed*. It, too, was a testimony against the anti-trinitarian heresies of the fourth and fifth centuries. Though setting forth the doctrines of Athanasius, the bishop of Alexandria, who died 373, this symbol was not written by this great defender of orthodoxy.

Modern scholars date its origin not earlier than about 450. The Athanasian Creed is perhaps the most explicit statement of the doctrine of the Trinity to be found in the literature of the Church. Rightly therefore the Lutheran Church has always held it in high esteem, and Luther himself says of it: "I doubt if since the days of the apostles anything more important has ever been written in the Church of the New Testament."

THE AUGSBURG CONFESSION

In addition to these three General Creeds, which the Lutheran Church has inherited from the ancient Church and adopted as her own, six other writings came into existence during Reformation times and soon after, which, by common consent, have come to be accepted as Lutheran Confessions, expressing the doctrine of the Lutheran Church. First and foremost among these is the Augsburg Confession, variously styled "the grand confession" ("Confessio augusta," a play on its Latin name Augustana), "the fundamental and chief confession of Evangelical Lutheran Christendom," etc. It received its name from the fact that it was presented to Emperor Charles V at the Diet of Augsburg in the year 1530. Upon issuing the summons for this diet in January of the same year, the emperor had called upon the Lutheran princes to present to him, on that occasion, a statement relative to the innovations in faith which they had instituted in their several countries. Melanchthon, utilizing certain articles that had been previously drawn up by Luther and others, elaborated the 28 articles composing the Confession, which in a masterly way set forth and defend the evangelical standpoint, and refute the errors and abuses of the Roman Catholic Church, from which the Evangelicals found it necessary to dissent. The document received the unqualified approval of Luther, who wrote about it in his celebrated letter of May 15, 1530: "I have read Master Philip's Apology. It pleases me very well, and I know nothing to improve nor change; nor would it be appropriate, since I cannot step so gently and softly. Christ, our Lord, help that it may bring much and great fruit, as we hope and pray. Amen."

The Augsburg Confession was written in the German and Latin languages. Both copies were signed by the Lutheran princes and the magistrates of two free cities, and it was agreed to present them as the common confession of the Protestant party. The 25th of June, 1530, was the memorable day on which the noble Confession was, by Chancellor Beyer, in the German language, publicly read before the Emperor and the diet. Both copies were delivered to Charles, who kept the Latin and gave the German to the Archbishop of Meinz to be deposited in the archives of the empire.

The reading of the Confession made a profound impression, not only on the Protestants, but even on many of the opposing Catholic party. Bishop Stadion of Augsburg exclaimed: "What has been read is the pure truth, and we cannot deny it." And when Eck told Duke William of Bavaria, who complained that he had been misinformed as to the Lutheran doctrine, that he was able to refute the Augustana with the Fathers, but not with the Holy Scriptures, William replied: "So, indeed, I hear that the Lutherans are sitting in the Scriptures and we, who follow the Pontiff, outside of it." And ever since the time of its solemn presentation the Augustana has obtained as the great and fundamental confession of the Lutheran Church throughout the world.

As regards its contents, the Augsburg Confession is divided into two parts. The first part embraces 21 articles, treating the fundamental doctrines of the evangelical faith, such as the doctrine of God (Art. 1), of original sin (Art. 2), of justification (Art. 3), of Baptism (Art. 9), of the Lord's Supper (Art. 10), of faith and good works (Art. 20), and others. The second part contains 7 articles, "concerning which there is dissension, and in which are related the abuses which have been corrected." Here we find discussed, e. g. (in Art. 22), the question of administering both elements to the laity in Communion, of the marriage of priests (in Art. 23), of the Mass (Art. 24), etc., all matters which were at issue between the Protestants and the Catholics at that time. It will at once be seen, however, from this partial table of contents, that the questions discussed, doctrinal as well as practical, are still of vital, fundamental importance for the Church of Christ, and must remain such for all time to come.

One brief historical note touching the Augustana remains to be made. In a later edition of the Latin text of the Confession, which Melanchthon issued in 1540, he introduced several textual changes, especially in the tenth article on the Lord's Supper, designed to make concessions to the Reformed party. For that reason it has become necessary and customary to distinguish between the two editions, and Lutherans, in designating their confessional standpoint, declare their adherence to the Unaltered Augsburg Confession as it is contained in the Book of Concord of 1580.

The Apology

The second of the Lutheran Symbols is the Apology of the Augsburg Confession. As its name implies, it was intended to be a defense of the Augustana. It was called forth by the Roman Catholic Confutation, a writing drawn up by more than twenty Catholic theologians, at the behest of Emperor Charles V, in answer to the document which the Lutherans had presented to the diet. The first draft of this Confutation, which, instead of refuting the Augustana, reviled and slandered Luther, was angrily rejected by the Emperor and the Catholic princes, and only after it had been rewritten five times was it finally read to the diet. Yet, after all this travailing of the mountains, the proverbial mouse was brought forth, that is to say, the Confutation was a pitiable excuse of a counter-argument. Still the Emperor and his party declared that the Lutherans had been refuted, and demanded their unconditional submission. This they refused, and requested a copy of the Confutation for the purpose of preparing a reply. When they were denied even this, Melanchthon, with the aid of other Lutheran theologians, set to work to prepare their reply on the basis of notes which Camerarius and others had taken during the reading of the Confutation.

This first draft of the Apology was presented to the diet on the 22d of September, but permission to read it was refused, nor was it received by the Emperor. It was afterwards, when also a copy of the Confutation had been obtained, rewritten and materially enlarged by Melanchthon. The Latin edition was published in the spring of 1531 together with the Augsburg Confession. The German edition, a free translation prepared by Justus Jonas and revised by Melanchthon, appeared in the fall of the same year. Though Melanchthon had not been authorized to rewrite the Apology, it was recognized by the Lutheran princes and theologians in 1532 at the convent in Schweinfurt as their confession, and in 1537, at Smalcald, by order of the princes, subscribed to by 32 representative Lutheran divines. In 1580 it was incorporated in the Book of Concord.

THE SMALCALD ARTICLES

Next in succession among the Lutheran Confessions are the Smalcald Articles, so called because they were adopted at the city of that name during an important convention of Lutherans held there in the year 1537. They were called forth by a summons issued by the Pope for a general council of the Church to be opened on May 8, 1537, at Mantua, in northern Italy. The Elector of Saxony, the leader among the evangelical princes of Germany, at once requested Luther to draw up a confession to be presented to the council, in which the attitude of the Protestants towards Rome should be restated in clearer and stronger terms than in the Augsburg Confession. Luther finished his articles toward the end of December, 1536. And having been signed in Wittenberg by Luther, Jonas, Melanchthon, Spalatin, Amsdorf, and Agricola, the document was sent to the Elector at the beginning of the year 1537. The Elector, in a letter of January 7, thanked Luther, and expressed his entire satisfaction with the articles. In Smalcald they were signed by the Lutheran theologians, the total number of subscriptions amounting to 44. The Smalcald Articles were incorporated in the Book of Concord of 1580 as a repetition and explanation of the Augsburg Confession and as a statement why the Lutherans abandoned the papistical errors and idolatries.

The Smalcald Articles consist of three main parts. The first part, in four brief articles, treats the doctrine of the Holy Trinity and the person of Christ. About these the Confession itself says: "There is no dispute nor contention about these articles; and inasmuch as both parties confess them, it is unnecessary now to treat further of them." Part two, the principal part of the Confession, contains four articles that treat the fundamental differences between Lutherans and papists, *viz.*, salvation alone by faith in Christ, the Mass, convents, and the Pope's authority. The third part embraces thirteen articles, discussing mostly doctrinal questions, such as sin, the Law, the Gospel, the Sacraments, etc., "all matters about which the Pope and the papal government do not care much. For with them conscience is nothing, but money, glory, honors, powers, are to them everything."

Besides these three parts there is an appendix, a "Treatise on the Power and Primacy of the Pope." It was drawn up at Smalcald by Melanchthon, at the instance of the Lutheran princes, who wished to state clearly their position with reference to the papacy, which "for reasons" had been omitted in the Augsburg Confession of 1530. As the Smalcald Articles bear the unmistakable imprint of Luther's heroic spirit and powerful diction, so the "Treatise" shows Melanchthon's thorough knowledge and happy way of objective presentation.

LUTHER'S CATECHISMS

The Small and Large Catechisms of Luther, which follow the Smalcald Articles in the Book of Concord, owing to the date of their formal acceptance by the Church as confessional writings, were written in the year 1529, earlier than any of the other Symbolical Books. It is scarcely necessary to say much about these two, particularly the former, because it is a household book in every Lutheran home and also well known outside of Lutheran circles.

The occasion and purpose of the Small Catechism Luther himself sets forth in the preface to it with these words: "The deplorable destitution which I recently observed during a visitation of the churches has impelled and constrained me to prepare this Catechism, or Christian Doctrine, in such a small and simple form. Alas, what manifold misery I beheld! The common people, especially in the villages, know nothing at all of Christian doctrine; and many pastors are quite unfit and incompetent to teach. Yet all are called Christians, have been baptized, and enjoy the use of the Sacraments, although they know neither the Lord's Prayer, nor the Creed, nor the Ten Commandments, and live like the poor brutes and irrational swine." The Catechism was written to remedy this deplorable condition of ignorance by serving pastors as a brief compendium for instructing the young and ignorant in the chief articles of the Christian religion. And this purpose it fulfils in an admirable manner. It sets forth the great vital truths of Christianity in a simple and, withal, sublime way, so that every child can grasp them. Hence this Catechism has been rightly styled "The layman's Bible," and to this day holds the first place among Lutheran text-books of instruction for the young, not only among German Lutherans, but those of all nationalities, for it has been translated, along with the Bible, into every language in which Lutheran doctrine is proclaimed.

In the Preface to his Large Catechism Luther says: "But this I say for myself. I am also a doctor and a preacher, yea, as learned and experienced as all who have such presumption and security. Yet I do as a child who is being taught the Catechism. Every morning, and whenever I have time, I read and say, word for word, the Ten Commandments, the Creed, the Lord's Prayer, the Psalms, etc. And I must still read and study daily, and yet I cannot master it as I wish, but must remain, and that too gladly, a child and a pupil of the Catechism." Mathesius said: "The world can never sufficiently thank and repay Luther for his little Catechism." Justus Jonas remarked: "It may be bought for sixpence, but six thousand worlds would not pay for it."

Also by non-Lutherans much has been said in praise of Luther's Small Catechism. McGiffert, the president of Union Theological Seminary, has called it "the Gem of the Reformation." Philip Schaff wrote in *The Creeds of Christendom*: "Luther's Small Catechism is truly a great little book, with as many thoughts as words, and every word telling and sticking to the heart as well as the memory. It bears the stamp of the religious genius of Luther, who was both its father and its pupil. It exhibits his almost apostolic gift of expressing the deepest things in the plainest language for the common people. It is strong food for a man, and yet as simple as a child. It marks an epoch in the history of religious instruction: it purged it from popish superstitions, and brought it back to Scriptural purity and simplicity. As it left far behind all former catechetical manuals, it has, in its own order of excellence and usefulness, never been surpassed. In the age of the Reformation it was an incalculable blessing. Luther himself wrote no better book, excepting, of course, his translation of the Bible, and it alone would have immortalized him as one of the great benefactors of the human race. Few books have elicited such enthusiastic praise, and have even to this day such grateful admirers."

Luther's genius shows itself no less in the selection than in the arrangement and treatment of the material that composes the Small Catechism. The selection is masterly, embracing in five parts all the essential truths of Christianity; the doctrine of God, of the sinfulness and lost condition of man, of his redemption by Christ and adoption as God's child, of the application of this salvation by the Holy Spirit through the means of grace and the exercise of his filial privileges in prayer. No less masterly is the arrangement: first the Ten Commandments, the Law, "the schoolmaster to bring the sinner to Christ"; then the Apostles' Creed, the Gospel, placing the doctrines of God, of His relation to man, the redemption of Christ, and the work of the Spirit, in the very center; after that, in the exposition of the Lord's Prayer, the Christian's privilege as a child to pray to his heavenly Father; and finally, as a kind of supplement, the doctrine of the Sacraments, the seals of his redemption and adoption.

Finally also the treatment is masterfully executed. To exemplify: In the commandments, Luther, following the example of the New Testament, excluded everything that had reference only to the Old Dispensation, thus in his wording of the First, Third, and Fourth Commandments, as also in the explanation of the Third; most beautifully he points out the only source from which a right and proper fulfilment of the Law must flow by the introductory words to the explanation of all the commandments, to wit, the fear and love of God. In the second part his explanations of the Three Articles are "veritable trumpet-blasts," setting forth the great works of God, creation, redemption, and sanctification, "as the fundamental facts of our salvation; not, however, as purely objective, abstract, doctrinal statements, but with all the fervor of personal conviction and appropriation."—From every point of comparison Luther's Catechism is vastly superior to the catechisms of other churches. (One point of difference between Luther's Catechism and those of other churches which should be briefly noticed here is his arrangement of the Commandments. He has exscinded the prohibition of graven images [Ex. 20:4, 5], because this evidently forms only a part of the First Commandment, while the Reformed catechisms make this the Second Commandment, so that from that commandment on their numeration differs from ours.)

Of the Large Catechism very little need be said, since in its general arrangement it follows exactly the order of the Small Catechism, and, as the name indicates, is only a more detailed and exhaustive discussion of the five chief parts of Christian doctrine which compose the former, designed for more advanced Christians. Both of Luther's catechisms form a valuable addition to the confessional writings of our Church. In the Formula of Concord they were endorsed as follows: "Lastly, because these highly important matters belong also to the common people and laity, who, for their salvation, must distinguish between pure and false doctrine, we accept as confessional also the Large and Small Catechisms of Dr. Luther, as they were written by him and incorporated in his works, because they have been unanimously approved and received by all churches adhering to the Augsburg Confession, and publicly used in churches, schools, and [privately in] families, and because also in them the Christian doctrine from God's Word is comprised in the most correct and simple way, and, in like manner, is sufficiently explained for simple laymen."

The Formula of Concord

One more of the Lutheran Symbols remains to be spoken of, the Formula of Concord, the last of them not only in their order of succession, but also in the time of its composition, having been completed in 1577, three years before the final publication of the Book of Concord. It originated in the attempt of a number of prominent Lutheran clergymen, among whom were Jacob Andreae, Martin Chemnitz, and Nicholas Selnecker, to settle the controversies which had arisen after Luther's death in 1546, and which had been sorely distracting the Lutheran Church for several decades. The Formula was the result of a combination and repeated careful revision of a series of theological documents. The final revision was made 1576 at Cloister Bergen, near Magdeburg. By agreement of the Lutheran princes the authentic edition of the Formula of Concord, together with the other Lutheran Symbols, was published on the 25th day of June, 1580, the semi-centennial of the glorious public presentation and reading of the Augsburg Confession at the Diet of Augsburg.

The Formula of Concord is essentially a restatement of the principal Lutheran doctrines, discussed already in the previously written and adopted Confessions. In a sermon delivered 1579, Jacob Andreae truly said of the Formula: "It is, in reality, nothing but Luther's Catechism." Owing to its purpose of settling controversies within the Lutheran Church, it is naturally very explicit and complete in its statement of the doctrines at issue. It consists of two main parts, the Epitome, a summary or definition, as the name implies, of the disputed articles of doctrine, and the *Solida Declaratio*, a full discussion of these same articles. Each contains an introduction on the Holy Scriptures as the sole rule of faith, and on the Lutheran confessions as testimonies to such faith, and twelve chapters on: Original Sin, The Free Will, The Righteousness of Faith before God, Good Works, The Law and the Gospel, The Third Use of the Law, The Lord's Supper, The Person of Christ, The Descent of Christ to Hell, Church Ceremonies, God's Eternal Predestination and Election, and Other Heretics and Sectarians. The most important of these articles are those on the Lord's Supper and the Person of Christ, the former showing the implicit faith of the Lutheran Church in the plain Word of God, the latter victoriously and consistently maintaining the personal unity, the true deity, and infinite sacrifice of Christ, the God-man.—

Such is a hurried outline of the confessional Books of the Lutheran Church, in which she has laid down, for all time to come, her official standpoint on all matters of doctrine, and by which she distinguishes herself from all other churches. In them she possesses a treasure of which she is justly proud, and every Lutheran Christian should make it his aim to become thoroughly conversant with their contents. The closing paragraph of the Formula of Concord shows how Lutherans treasure, and the spirit in which they receive, their confessions. It reads as follows: "Therefore in the sight of God and of all Christendom (the entire Church of Christ), to those now living and those who shall come after us, we wish to testify that the above declaration concerning all the controverted articles presented and explained, and no other, is our faith, doctrine, and confession, in which we also will appear, by God's grace, with unterrified hearts before the judgment-seat of Jesus Christ, and for it will give an account. We also will neither speak nor write, privately or publicly, anything contrary to this declaration, but, by the help of God's grace, intend to abide thereby. After mature deliberation we have, in God's fear and with the invocation of His name, attached our signatures with our own hands."

PART III

Distinctive Practices and Customs of the Lutheran Church

The principal, most essential point of difference between the Lutheran Church and other churches that bear the name Christian are its distinctive doctrines, by which it is separated from the latter. However, there are also other points of distinction, which are no less marked, though not so vital and essential as the foregoing. The Lutheran Church observes and maintains certain time-honored customs and practices, which are in part based directly upon Scriptural command or precedent, though perhaps not enjoined by God in just the form in which we have them; while in part they are of merely human, ecclesiastical origin, and are therefore not considered binding in any sense, but are nevertheless cherished as valuable outward marks of distinction between Lutherans and non-Lutherans.

Sponsors

A number of these distinctive Lutheran practices cluster about the administration of the

Sacraments, and we shall take these up first as being among the most important ones. With reference to *Baptism*, the Lutheran Church has retained the ancient ecclesiastical customs of having sponsors, or godparents, at the baptism of young children. The purpose for which sponsors are employed is a threefold one: 1) They are to be witnesses of the fact that the child has been baptized; 2) they are representatives of the child in the solemn rite and answer in its place; 3) they assume responsibility, next to its parents, for its Christian training in the doctrines of the Lutheran Church. It lies in the nature of the case that only Lutherans in good standing should be chosen for this important function, and that those not in the fellowship of the faith may be admitted only as witnesses, but not as sponsors proper.

This is indeed not a distinctively Lutheran custom in the sense that sponsors are employed in the Lutheran Church only. For also the Roman Catholic and Greek Churches have them, and also some other Protestant churches. But the Lutheran Church has restored this custom to its proper form, and purified it of the abuses that had gathered also around it in the Roman Catholic Church, which, *e. g.*, maintains that such a close spiritual relationship is established between godparent and godchild that marriage between them is not permissible!

The sponsors, it has been remarked, are to answer certain questions in the name of the child during the rite of Baptism. In the Lutheran formulas of Baptism the person to be baptized is asked to "renounce the devil and all his works and all his ways," and to confess his faith in the Triune

God as expressed in the Apostles' Creed. This is not merely a symbolical act, according to the Lutheran view of the matter. As has been shown under the doctrine of Baptism, this Sacrament is not merely a symbol of the establishment of the covenant relation between God and the baptized person, but the effectual means of establishing this relation. Now with reference to circumcision, the Old Testament type of Baptism, God had distinctly told Abraham at the time of its institution: "The uncircumcised man-child, whose flesh of his foreskin is not circumcised, that soul shall be cut off from his people; he has broken My covenant." (Gen. 17:14.) Here it is said of the uncircumcised child that he has broken God's covenant, and was to be punished for it; so, of course, the reverse is also true: by circumcision the child entered into the covenant of God. Thus also in Baptism, the antitype of circumcision, our children enter into covenant-relation with God, and sever their relation with Satan, in whose kingdom they were by nature. Renunciation of the devil and profession of faith in the Triune God are therefore not a mere matter of form, but are an expression of realities. The baptismal vow, expressed in the place of the child by the sponsors, is therefore not a mere formality, but a solemn obligation contracted by the baptized infant through the sponsors that take its place.

CLOSE COMMUNION

In the administration of the Lord's Supper the Lutheran Church has adopted the practice of close communion, *i.e.*, of admitting to her altars only such as are of the fellowship of faith, or fellow-Lutherans in good standing. She bases this practice upon the Scriptural teaching that partaking of Holy Communion is an act of confession, in a wider sense, a confession of faith in Christ, in a limited sense also confession of the faith of that particular Church in which one partakes of the Sacrament. The former is plainly taught by St. Paul, when he writes (1 Cor. 11:26): "As often as ye eat this bread, and drink this cup, ye do show forth the Lord's death," *i.e.*, partaking of the Lord's Supper is a showing forth, a proclaiming of the sacrificial death of Christ, is a solemn confession: I am a believer in Christ and His redemption.— Another passage in point is 1 Cor. 10:17: "For we, being many, are one bread and one body; for we are all partakers of that one bread." By communing together, we confess or acknowledge ourselves as members of one body, as brethren in the faith. And the same idea we find expressed in a different way, in Acts 2:42: "And they continued steadfastly in the apostles' doctrine and *fellowship*, and in breaking of bread, and in prayer." Breaking bread, *i. e.*, partaking of the Lord's Supper, with others, means fellowship in the faith, that is to say, those with whom we commune we acknowledge as being of the same faith with ourselves. To commune with those of another church therefore implies that we recognize their faith to be the same as ours, that our differences amount to nothing and may safely be ignored, which for a confessional Lutheran is tantamount to saying that the teachings of the Word of God may be set aside.

Thus the confessional Lutheran Church excludes from its altars not only the openly wicked and unbelieving, of whom we may be sure that they would "eat and drink damnation to themselves, not discerning the Lord's body" (1 Cor. 11:29), but also the heterodox, *i. e.*, those of another faith than our own, for reasons outlined above. Most Reformed churches, on the other hand, practice "open communion," inviting all Christians, all members of any Christian church, to their altars. And strangely enough, they seemingly use the same argument for their position that we Lutherans use for ours. They say that, since it is the Lord's table, no man has a right to keep away a disciple of the Lord, no matter to what church he belongs; while Lutherans argue that, because it is the Lord's table, we have no right to admit any one and every one to it, but must administer the Sacrament in accordance with the Master's instructions.—It should also be noted that, in conformity with this divergent view of the Sacrament, also different modes of its administration have developed. In the Lutheran Church the communicants approach the altar in groups, and there receive the consecrated elements; in most "open communion" churches the elements are passed by the deacons among the audience in the pews, and whoever desires partakes of them.

ANNOUNCEMENT

An outgrowth of the practice of "close communion" in the Lutheran Church is the system of "announcement," which means that those wishing to partake of Communion are expected to record their names with the pastor beforehand, so that he, who "watches over their souls as he that must give account," may be enabled to see to it that none are admitted to the holy table of whom he is convinced that they are unfit to partake of it, in order that "that which is holy may not be given to the dogs, and the pearls may not be cast before swine" (Matt. 7:6). Although this practice is not based upon a direct word of God, yet it is most certainly a blessed and salutary institution, by means of which much good is accomplished and much harm averted.

CONFESSION AND ABSOLUTION

A very important rite, invariably observed in Lutheran churches in connection with the celebration of Holy Communion, is that of confession and absolution. In a special preparatory service, held previous to the Communion services, either on the same or the preceding day, the communicants gather in the church, and, after listening to a confessional address by the pastor, make confession of their sins, and are then absolved by him, *i.e.*, assured of the forgiveness of their sins "in the stead and by the command of the Lord Jesus Christ." While there is no direct command of Christ or His apostles for the observance of this solemn rite in connection with Communion, it has been in vogue in the Church since its earliest days, and it is most certainly a very salutary institution, for it emphasizes, as

G . L u e c k e | 89

nothing else could, the main purpose for which we partake of the Lord's Supper, *viz.*, to receive renewed assurance of the forgiveness of our sins. In the Papal Church its observance had degenerated into the doctrine of auricular confession, which makes it obligatory upon every one of its members to confess his sins to the priest, and conditions the forgiveness of sins upon such confession and the priest's absolution. Luther, the conservative Reformer, retained the rite itself as a blessed and salutary one, merely purging it of the abuses which had crept into its observance. Following Zwingli and Calvin, the iconoclastic reformers, the other Protestant Churches, with the exception of the Episcopal Church, have cast it overboard entirely. And very naturally so, for they deny that Christ has delegated the power of forgiving sins to men, while the Lutheran Church, on the basis of plain Scripture-passages, maintains that He has done so. Let me quote only the two most important ones, both of them words of the Savior Himself. The first is Matt. 18:18, where He says of His Christians: "Verily, verily, I say unto you, Whatsoever ye shall bind on earth shall be bound in heaven, and whatsoever ye shall loose on earth shall be loosed in heaven." The second is John 20:23: "Receive the Holy Spirit: whosesoever sins you remit, they are remitted unto them; and whosesoever sins you retain, they are retained."

THE WAFER

Another point of difference between the Lutheran and Reformed mode of administering the

Lord's Supper is the retention of the wafer by the former. The wafer, or host, is unleavened bread, baked in the form of small round wafers, just the proper size to be received by the communicant. It was introduced in the Catholic Church during the Middle Ages and retained by Luther. The Reformed Churches, on the other hand, mostly use ordinary leavened bread, which is broken by the pastor into small particles to symbolize the breaking of Christ's body. Lutherans consider this breaking unnecessary, because Christ, during the institution, merely broke it in order to reduce it to the proper shape for reception by the disciples. (The unleavened bread used by the Jews during the Passover was similar to our crackers, and therefore could not well be reduced to small bits except by being broken.) While Lutherans do not condemn the use of other bread, they as emphatically maintain their right to use the bread baked in the form of wafers, and retain its use as a distinctively Lutheran custom; nor will they allow themselves to be frightened out of its use by the cry that this is "Catholic." Luther retained the wafer, which he found in use in the Roman Catholic Church, because of its convenient form, and because he saw no objection to its use, and it has become one of the distinctive usages of the Church bearing his name, because the Reformed Churches base their use of ordinary bread upon a false interpretation of Scripture, *viz.*, the assumption that the bread in Communion must be broken to typify the breaking of Christ's body on the cross, an assumption that is squarely controverted by Scripture, which expressly denies such a breaking of His body. (Compare John 19:33–36.)

Parochial Schools

The Lutheran Church also distinguishes itself from most of the other Protestant Churches by the way in which she educates her young members, and prepares them for, and receives them into, full membership. The Lutheran Church has always laid great stress upon the necessity of a thorough Christian education and indoctrination of its children. And to give them this, she has adopted the Christian parochial school as the best means available under conditions in which she must carry on the work of her Lord in this country. While making use of the Sunday-school, primarily as a missionary institution, she is not satisfied with it alone for its children, but regards it as insufficient by itself to give the Christian training demanded by the Word of God. All other Protestant Churches, on the contrary, content themselves with the Sunday-school, and the very limited instruction in religious truths which it can give.

Catechetical Instruction

Nor is the Lutheran Church content with the Christian training and education which it affords its children in the daily parish-school, where circumstances at all permit this. She furthermore supplements this by a thorough course of catechetical instruction, imparted to them by the pastor preparatory to confirmation. The purpose of this is to ground them still more firmly in the essentials of the faith before they are admitted to the full enjoyment of all church-privileges, in particular to the partaking of Holy Communion. The Protestant denominations in our country, with the possible exception of the German Reformed and Evangelical Churches, know nothing of such a course of catechetical instruction. To this absence of thorough religious instruction and training is due, in large measure, the woeful religious ignorance and the irreligious character of so large a portion of our population. Instead of the thorough religious training of the young, these churches mostly employ the high-pressure methods of revivalism for the gaining of converts and enlarging of their membership.

CONFIRMATION

In the preceding paragraphs allusion has already been made to another Lutheran usage, closely allied with what has just now been discussed—the rite of Confirmation. While not of divine, but only of human, ecclesiastical origin, Confirmation has come down to us from the early centuries of the Christian era, and Luther, true to his principles, took it over from the Roman Catholic Church, minus the superstitious abuses that had clustered about it in that Church. For while Catholics regard it as a sacrament, it is to Lutherans merely a personal renewal of the baptismal covenant prior to admission to the Lord's Table, and withal a time-honored and effective means of impressing upon young

Christians the sanctity of this covenant. Confirmation is indeed not an exclusively Lutheran custom. Not only the Roman Catholic Church, as already noted, but also several Protestant denominations have it, *e. g.*, the Episcopal and the Reformed and German Evangelical Churches. And, indeed, the latter observe it in much the same manner and for the same purpose as the Lutheran Church. While in these churches the pastors administer the rite, this function in the two former churches is reserved to the bishops. The other American churches have all dispensed with it altogether, as well as with the preparatory catechetical instruction, admitting adult or adolescent members either by baptism, as in the Baptist denominations, or by mere confession of faith, as in the Methodist, Presbyterian, and other churches.

ORDINATION

With regard to the ministerial office and its functions, several customs prevail in the Lutheran Church that we must briefly notice in this connection. One of these is the rite of ordination, *i. e.*, the solemn setting aside for, and induction of, a person into the sacred office by prayer and the laying on of hands. The Lutheran Church, indeed, does not consider ordination an essential prerequisite for the performance of ministerial functions because there is no command for it in the Scripture. All that is essentially necessary for that is the call. Thus the Augsburg Confession says: "No one may teach publicly in the Church, or administer the Sacraments, except he be rightly called." And Luther says: "He who is called is consecrated, and may preach to him who gave the call. That is our Lord's consecration." But while there is no Scriptural command for ordination, there is abundant Scriptural precedent for it. (See Acts 6:5, 6; 13:1, 3; 1 Tim. 4:14; 5:22.) And therefore ordinarily no one would be permitted to hold the ministerial office in the Lutheran Church without having previously received ordination.

This rite of ordination, based as it is upon Scriptural precedent, has universally prevailed in the Christian Church since its earliest days, and it is in vogue in nearly all branches of the Church at this day, with important differences, however, in its administration. In the Roman and Greek Churches it is considered a sacrament, and is supposed to confer an indelible character ("Once a priest, always a priest"); and in the former it can be administered only by a bishop. The Episcopal Church also restricts this function to the bishops, but does not consider it a sacrament. In the Presbyterian Church it is conferred by the presbyters. In the Lutheran Church it is looked upon as the public attestation of the church that the candidate is duly qualified and called to the holy office; hence it is conferred in its name by the officers of the church (with us by the synodical presidents), or, under due authorization from them, by any pastor in their stead.

THE CLERICAL GOWN

While we are speaking of the ministry, we may also notice that it is customary in most of the Lutheran churches for the preacher to wear a gown, or robe, during the public services of the church. Special clerical vestments were introduced in the New Testament Church in accordance with Old Testament precedent. (See Ex. 40:13 ff.; Lev. 8:7 ff., for the holy garments of the Jewish high priest.) The clerical vestments, with the development of the sacerdotal idea, became more and more elaborate. Luther declared them to be non-essential, but in accordance with the general conservative tendency of his Reformation their use was generally retained in the Lutheran Church; but with the repudiation of the priestly character of the clergy they were greatly simplified. And so the plain black robe, still worn to-day by a majority of Lutheran pastors, became the rule. To this were added, in the course of years, the white bands worn around the neck, which is merely a somewhat altered relic of the peculiar kind of lace collar worn by men during a part of the seventeenth century. No particular significance is, therefore, attached to either one of these by Lutherans beyond their purpose of distinguishing, or setting aside, the person of the called minister from the lay congregation. And while a somewhat similar form of gown is also worn by some ministers in the Presbyterian Church, the clerical robe is, to a large extent, a distinctive characteristic of the Lutheran Church.

ALTAR AND PULPIT

This discussion of the ministerial robe leads us to that of other matters connected with the Lutheran mode of worship.—Already the style of architecture in Lutheran churches, largely retained from its ancient style preserved in Roman Catholic churches, differs from that of other Protestant churches, and adapts itself to the peculiarly Lutheran manner of worship. The Lutheran Church has retained the altar and the closed pulpit, whereas other Protestants have substituted for the former a table and for the latter the desk-pulpit or pulpit-stand. In a Lutheran church the altar—over which, in the Holy of Holies, the Lord was present in His glory—symbolizes God's presence to His children. It therefore occupies the most prominent position, in the center of the fore part. In prayer, therefore, the pastor turns towards it, while in addressing the congregation and pronouncing the benediction he faces the congregation. At the altar, too, the Sacrament of the Lord's Supper is fitly celebrated, which is therefore also designated "The Sacrament of the Altar" by Luther's Small Catechism, for it is a memento of Christ's sacrificial death upon the altar of the cross. On the altar are placed candlesticks, which during the celebration of the Sacrament are lighted, recalling to mind the fact that it is the Lord's Supper, instituted in the night in which He was betrayed. Also a crucifix is generally found on it, as a continuous reminder of Christ's great sacrifice on Calvary.—The pulpit is usually placed to one side of the altar, and its enclosed form, like the gown, is designed to conceal the person of the preacher, emphasizing the truth that he stands there in the place, as the mouthpiece, of Christ.—Another piece of furniture, customarily found in Lutheran churches is the baptismal font, placed, as a rule, on the side of the altar opposite to the pulpit. It is rightly placed close to the altar, in the view of the congregation, and—to mention it in passing—it emphasizes the truth that the church and the public service is the proper place and time also for the administration of this Sacrament.

THE SIGN OF THE CROSS

Passing on now to certain customs that prevail in Lutheran worship, we notice, first, the retention of the sign of the cross in connection with Baptism and the Lord's Supper and also the benediction. This, as well as the crucifix and the use of candles and wafers in the celebration of Communion, is often denounced as a relic of Romanism. But Luther and the Lutheran Church have divested these things of Roman Catholic superstitions and abuses. Thus the sign of the cross, which to a devout Catholic is often a sort of charm with a magic power to protect against danger and harm, is to the Lutheran a mere reminder of Christ's redemptive suffering and death. And why should it be wrong to employ it as such a reminder?

SET FORMS OF PRAYERS

Another very prominent feature of Lutheran worship is the extensive use of set forms of prayer, i. e., prayers which are read from a book by the pastor, instead of free, *ex corde* prayers, almost exclusively employed in other Protestant churches. These read prayers are often belittled, because it is claimed that they too easily degenerate into a mere recital of the mouth, without due devotion of the heart. No doubt, there is some truth in this claim. But does not the same hold good of that great model prayer which the Master Himself taught His disciples to pray? Indeed, Luther rightly styles this prayer the "greatest martyr," because it is so often repeated thoughtlessly and listlessly. And on the other hand, is there not abundant evidence that the free, *ex corde* prayer only too often degenerates into that use of "vain repetitions" against which the Savior Himself warns us?—Not only in public worship, but also in private devotion, Lutherans largely use the printed prayers. Hence the Lutheran Church possesses, besides a wealth of other devotional books, also a large number of prayer-books for private use, containing many model prayers by great masters of prayer. While encouraging the use, by her members, of such printed prayers, she by no means disparages the prayer that is a free outflow of the heart's devotion. (Other churches largely using the printed form of prayer are, besides the Catholic, the Episcopal churches.)—In this connection also a word about posture in prayer. While the Bible commands no special posture, it does mention and recommend several, *e.g.*, kneeling and "lifting up holy hands." Those in vogue in the Lutheran Church are: kneeling as an acknowledgment of unworthiness; standing, as a mark of reverence; and the folding of hands, as a token of helplessness and dependence on God.—In public worship the congregation also stands during the reading of the Scriptures, likewise as a token of reverence for the Word of God. Such expressions of reverence also are the bowing of the head in prayer and during the benediction, and the genuflection or bowing of the head at the approach to the Lord's Table.

Church-Year

Another feature of Lutheran worship by which it is distinguished from that of other church-bodies, with the exception of the Catholic and Episcopal Churches, is the observance of a so-called church-year. It does not lie within the province of this book to trace the development of this custom from the early days of the Church, nor to point out the unimportant divergences existing between the Lutheran and the Catholic and Episcopal church-year. We shall note only the outstanding features of its observance in the Lutheran Church. It begins with the first Sunday of Advent, four weeks before Christmas. As the name implies, these four Sundays are to prepare the Church for the advent, the coming of Christ into the flesh, which is celebrated on the joyous Christmas-festival. Eight days later, on New Year's Day, the Church commemorates the circumcision of the Christ-child, which signifies His voluntary submission to the Law for our sakes. This, again, is followed, six days later, by the Epiphany-festival, which commemorates the manifestation of the new-born King of the Jews to the Wise Men from the East. About three months later, on the Sunday after the first vernal full moon, comes the greatest

of all church-festivals, Easter, the festival of
Christ's resurrection. This is preceded, on Friday of
the same week, by Good Friday, the day of the
Lord's crucifixion and death; by Maundy
Thursday, on which the Lord's Supper was
instituted and the Savior was betrayed; by Palm
Sunday, when He made His last, triumphal entry
into the city of Jerusalem and the multitude spread
palm-branches on His road. This week is known as
Holy Week, and the six weeks before Easter,
beginning with Ash Wednesday, are observed as
the season of Lent. During this time special
services are held in which the grand theme of all
sermons is the passion and death of the Savior.—
Forty days after Easter occurs the festival of the
Ascension of Christ to heaven, followed in turn,
after ten days, by Whitsunday, or Pentecost (the
Greek word for "fiftieth," *viz.*, the fiftieth day after
Easter), in commemoration of the outpouring of
the Holy Spirit upon the disciples. One week after
Pentecost the Church observes Trinity Sunday, the
festival of the mystery of the "Trinity in Unity," of
the Triune God. Thus the Lutheran Church, by the
three great festivals of her church-year, celebrates
all the most important and outstanding deeds of
God for the redemption and salvation of the sinful
world, thereby bringing these great and ever new
themes again and again to the attention of the
Christians in her midst. Certainly, when
contemplating the exalted character of these
festivals, one is struck by their vast superiority
over such lately inaugurated ecclesiastical
celebrations as Mothers' Day, Go-to-Church
Sunday, and others!—Besides these great festivals,

also each Sunday of the church-year has its special name, some of them designated by the first word of the Latin introit, appointed by the early Church for each Sunday (such as "Judica," "Rogate," and others); a few are numbered backward from Easter ("Quinquagesima," "Sexagesima," "Septuagesima"); still others are numbered forward from a special Sunday (thus the Sundays of Advent and after Trinity).

CHURCH-HYMNS AND CHURCH-MUSIC

One more subject requires brief mention in this connection, that of church-hymns and church-music. The Lutheran Church, from its inception in the Reformation, has always been a singing Church. Luther himself was a great writer of church-hymns and of music for his hymns, and a number of other such writers followed him, so that there is a wealth of Lutheran hymnody, particularly in the German language. A creditable beginning has been made in our country of a translation of numerous gems into the language of our country. But the English-speaking Lutherans of America also largely utilize the many beautiful hymns that have originated in other churches.—In keeping with the general character of Lutheran worship also its church-hymns and -music are characterized by dignity and solemnity, which differentiate them from much of the modern church-music and singing, which is only too often very light and even inane in its character.

PART IV

Organization of the Lutheran Church

In every sphere of human activity a certain amount of organization of some character is necessary for successfully carrying on any kind of enterprise—in business, in government, in school, or any other work. Without organization of some kind there can be only confusion and failure. And the same holds good of church-work. Without organization of some character it would be simply impossible to carry on properly the great and important work of saving souls which God has committed to His Church. In the Old Testament, under the covenant of the Law, God had Himself prescribed, to the minutest details, the form of organization for His people. In the New Testament, under the Gospel-covenant, He has left the character which this organization is to assume to the enlightened choice of the Church itself. Nevertheless the New Testament Scriptures indicate that it is God's intention that some form of organization should prevail in His Church. This the Lutheran Church has always recognized. And while adapting the details to circumstances and surroundings, she, in accordance with her governing principle, closely follows the Scriptures, in as far as they lay down the general principles of church-organization and -government.

First, then, she holds to the Scriptural view that in the Church there is only one divinely instituted organization, to wit, the local congregation, and that in it are vested all the powers and prerogatives conferred by Christ upon His Church; that it is the sole ruling power in the Church. Compare Matt. 18:17–20, where Christ gives to the church, *i.e.*, the local congregation, v. 18, the power of the keys, the embodiment of all spiritual powers. See also 1 Cor. 1:2: "the church of God which is at Corinth"; Gal. 1:2: "the churches of Galatia"; Rev. 1:4: "the seven churches which are in Asia," and other passages. Furthermore, the Lutheran Church upholds the Scriptural principle that within the local congregation the governing power is to be in the hands of the male members. "For the husband is the head of the wife, even as Christ is the Head of the Church" (Eph. 5:23).

While the local congregation is the sole divinely instituted organization in the Church, it has been found useful, for carrying on the work of the Church at large, to form wider organizations. For in order to conduct this work, it is necessary to educate ministers and teachers, and to maintain colleges and seminaries for this purpose, to send out missionaries and support them, to publish church-papers, etc. And all these things could not be done properly by each congregation singly. Hence it has been found necessary to form aggregations of a number of congregations, and to combine their efforts and resources so as to make these things possible. In the Lutheran Church of America the synodical form has been generally adopted, that is to say, a larger or smaller number of congregations that find themselves one in the faith combine to form a synod. Since, however, the congregation has been endowed by Christ Himself with all spiritual powers and prerogatives, it follows that a synod, which is only a voluntary combination of autonomous congregations, cannot be a ruler of the congregations, cannot be a legislative, but only an advisory body, and can possess only such powers as are expressly delegated to it by the common consent of the congregations constituting it. Therefore also such resolutions and transactions of a synod as concern its vital interests, constitutional changes, questions affecting the form of organization, and the like, are submitted to the congregations for ratification. On the other hand, the congregations, while zealously guarding their God-given rights against synodical usurpation, willingly submit, according to the law of love, to all reasonable enactments of synod, and show their willingness to do their share in helping to carry them out. Furthermore, while synods are only human institutions and no congregation can therefore be compelled to unite with one, yet it should not capriciously stand aloof by itself, because by so doing it deprives itself of many blessings that flow from such larger fellowship, and is at least tempted to neglect important duties that it owes toward the Church and its work at large.

Another important purpose of synodical organization is the preservation of "the unity of the Spirit in the bond of peace" (Eph. 4:3), *i. e.*, of the unity of doctrine and practice in the Church at large. For this reason some of the synods make it a point to devote some time at their conventions to the discussion of doctrinal questions. Another very important means to this end is the formation within the synodical bounds of pastors' and teachers' conferences, which meet at stated times for the express purpose of discussing matters of doctrine and practice. Without doubt great blessings flow down upon the Church from these conferences.

In every form of organization some office or offices are necessary for carrying on its work. This is true also of the Church. In as far as it is an organization engaged in work among men here on earth, it must do this work by human agencies, and by methods adapted to its environments. The divine Founder of the Church recognized this necessity, and He Himself created the one office that is absolutely necessary for its well-being and growth, to wit, the office of the holy ministry. He chose the twelve apostles, and sent them out to preach in His name. And the Apostle Paul (himself called by a heavenly vision to this great office) writes (Eph. 4:11, 12): "Christ gave some, apostles; and some, prophets; and some, evangelists; and some, pastors and teachers; for the perfecting of the saints, for the work of the ministry, for the edifying of the body of Christ." The various offices here mentioned were in reality only different forms of the same office, that of the ministry of the

Word, some of them instituted merely to suit the particular needs of those early days. And while, with the ceasing of these particular needs, some of the forms of the office enumerated here have fallen into disuse, the office itself has remained as the one essential, divinely instituted office of the Church.

Besides this office of the ministry, the Church, in the exercise of its Christian liberty, early created other offices for the carrying on of the different lines of its work, just as necessity arose for them. Thus the first church at Jerusalem instituted the office of deacon, choosing seven men out of its midst to minister to the daily distribution of food among the disciples (Acts 5). And that there were also lay-elders in the early churches, who assisted the pastors in ruling the congregation, is evident from 1 Tim. 5:17: "Let the elders that rule well be counted worthy of double honor, especially they who labor in the Word and doctrine." Evidently a distinction is here made between those that merely "rule," and those who also "labor in the Word and doctrine," *i.e.*, the preachers. From all this two things are plain, then: All offices in the Church are either developments of, or derivations from, the office of the ministry, or they are mere human, ecclesiastical institutions. And in both instances the Church uses her liberty vouchsafed her by God under the Gospel-dispensation.

Also in this particular the Lutheran Church follows Scriptural precept and precedent. While recognizing and honoring the ministry of the Word as the one divinely instituted office of the Church, she avails herself of her God-given right to mold this office and to create others to suit the particular needs of time and place. Thus she has instituted, here in our country, the office of the parochial schoolteacher as a derivative of the ministerial office. Also the various offices necessary for the conduct of the Sunday-school must be regarded as subordinate branches of the ministry. Lutherans also have retained the office of lay-elder, of deacon, of trustee, and others. Since these are of human origin, it is, of course, left to the individual congregation to adapt these to its own particular needs.

Naturally it has been found necessary, in the wider, extra-congregational organization of the Church, to have other offices besides those limited to the congregation. And in the synodical organization of the Lutheran Church in our country these offices are, of course, created by the different synods to suit their varying needs, and their duties and powers are specified by the synodical constitutions. Among these the most common are the synodical presidents, vice-presidents, secretaries, and treasurers. Then there are various boards of administration, mission boards, boards of trustees, or directors for the various educational, charitable, and other institutions, etc.

In other countries the organization of the Lutheran Church has assumed various other forms, and this has naturally led to the creation of other offices. While it is not within the purpose and scope of this treatise to discuss these, perhaps a word should be said about the episcopal office in the Lutheran Church. This office of bishop is not rejected as though it were in itself something wrong. (See Art. 28 of the Augsburg Confession and the Appendix to the Smalcald Articles.) In some countries, for instance, in Sweden, the Lutheran Church therefore exists under this form of government. But the office, like others heretofore described, is held to be of human origin, and its authority limited by the Word of God and by mutual agreement.

In the organization of the modern church a number of auxiliary institutions have come to play quite an important part, such as Ladies' Aid Societies, Young People's Societies, Women's Missionary Societies, and the like. The Lutheran Church has not been backward in adopting these as valuable aids in the carrying on of her great work. But while encouraging them, she is zealously intent upon confining them to their proper sphere, and restraining them from encroaching in any way upon the powers and prerogatives of the congregation, as is not infrequently done by these organizations in other churches.

PART V

Divisions of the Lutheran Church in America

GENERAL LUTHERAN BODIES

THE SYNODICAL CONFERENCE

Of the two General Lutheran bodies, at present existing in the United States, the Synodical Conference is the oldest. It was formed in 1872 at Milwaukee, Wis., by the Synods of Ohio, Missouri, Wisconsin, Minnesota, Illinois, and the Norwegian Synod. Of these, the Ohio Synod and the Norwegian Synod have since withdrawn, while the Illinois Synod was merged into the Missouri Synod. The Synodical Conference is merely a federation of the synods belonging to it, formed for the purpose of maintaining "the unity of the Spirit in the bond of peace," *i.e.*, for preserving the unity of truly Lutheran doctrine and practice. Hence the principal work at its meetings, which occur every two years, and at which the synods are represented by clerical and lay delegates, is the discussion of doctrinal papers. The only work carried on by them conjointly is the mission among the colored race in our country. In the interest of this work two periodicals are published, to wit, the *Missionstaube* in German and the *Lutheran Pioneer* in English. According to the statistics for 1918 the Synodical Conference embraces 3,399 pastors, 5,551 congregations and preaching-stations, 1,255,033 souls, about 800,000 communicants, 1,962 parish-schools, 1,119 male teachers, 438 female teachers, and 1,150 pastors teaching, 102,955 pupils, 95,981 Sunday-school children.

The oldest and, by far, the largest of the synods connected with the Synodical Conference is the Missouri Synod. It was organized 1847 in Chicago. The elements that combined to form it came from Missouri, Ohio, and other States. The purpose for which they united was the formation of a truly confessional Lutheran body, in doctrine as well as in practice. The beginnings were small, only 16 congregations and 22 ministers forming the charter members of the organization. But the growth has been phenomenal, so that today, after 72 years of existence, it is the largest individual Lutheran synod in America. This wonderful growth, under God, is no doubt due chiefly to its unflinching confessionalism and adherence to pure standards of doctrine and practice, to its active work among the large number of German Lutheran immigrants, and to its zeal in establishing and maintaining Christian parochial schools.

The work of the Synod, originally exclusively German, has in most of its congregations become bilingual, while its English District (organized as the "English Conference of Missouri," later reorganized as "The English Synod of Missouri," and still later combined with the German body as its "English District") carries on its work entirely in the language of our country. Of the Synod's two theological seminaries, the Theoretical Seminary at St. Louis, and the Practical Seminary at Springfield, Ill., the former, with nearly 400 matriculated students, is the largest of its kind in the country. Apart from numerous colleges the Synod also maintains two Normal Schools, one at River Forest, Ill. (formerly located in Addison), the other at Seward, Nebr., where the teachers for its parish-schools are trained. The official organs are *Der Lutheraner* in German and *The Lutheran Witness* in English. In addition the Synod publishes *Lehre und Wehre, The Theological Quarterly*, and *Homiletic Magazine* (bilingual) for its pastors, *Das Schulblatt* for its teachers, and several smaller periodicals. Its great printing establishment, where these publications, together with numerous books, such as text-books for the parochial schools, religious and theological books and pamphlets, are issued, is Concordia Publishing House, located at St. Louis, Mo.

Besides its most important work, that among the immigrant German Lutherans in our country and Canada, the Missouri Synod labors among other immigrant races, the Poles, Italians, Slovaks, Jews, etc.; also among our North American Indians. It supports an extensive work among the Germans in Brazil and Argentina, South America. It has been active also in Germany, Denmark, and London, in Australia and New Zealand; and it carries on flourishing missions among the heathen of India and China.

Of the founders and leaders of the Missouri Synod the first place is, of course, occupied by Dr. C. F. W. Walther, one of the foremost Lutheran theologians of America, if not the foremost. Even prior to the organization of the Synod he had been the recognized leader among the Saxon congregations in Missouri, the founder and editor of *Der Lutheraner*, and two years later he was elected professor of theology at the Seminary in St. Louis. He was also the leading spirit in the formation of the Synod; he drafted its first constitution, and thus laid down the basic principles of its organization. And he retained this leadership until his death. He was not only a great organizer, but a deep and soundly Lutheran theologian, a thorough student of the works of Luther and the older Lutheran theologians, a writer, teacher, and preacher of rare powers. He died in 1887.—Besides Walther we must at least mention F. W. Wyneken, the great pioneer and missionary of the early days of the Missouri Synod.

In his *Lutherans in America* (p. 421) Dr. Wolf describes the doctrinal and confessional attitude of the Missouri Synod as follows: "Here, then, was a Lutheran synod which declared in its constitution that the acceptance of all the Symbols of the Lutheran Church without exception or reserve, abstinence from every kind of syncretism, from mixed congregations and mixed services and communions, a permanent, not temporary or licensed, ministry, the use of purely Lutheran books in churches and schools, should be and remain conditions of membership with this body, but which, on the other hand, claimed no authority over the congregations connected with it, thus leaving intact the freedom of the churches." This strict confessional and conservative position assumed by the Missouri Synod and the synods affiliated with it in the Synodical Conference has unquestionably been the chief factor in promoting the tendency towards a purer and stricter Lutheranism, and served as a barrier against the spread of liberalism in other Lutheran synods of the country.

This feature is well brought out by an article entitled, "Fifty Years of Conservative Lutheranism," by "A Lutheran Correspondent," published in the New York *Independent*, April 29, 1897, the year of the Missouri Synod's fiftieth anniversary. Says the article in part: "In the entire length and breadth of this Church, contrary to the spirit and tendencies characteristic of other leading denominations, there has been, in the last generation, a pronounced conservative development, a revival of the confessional principle, a seeking after the ways of the Fathers in faith and worship. It is certainly a remarkable phenomenon that in an era when the general tendencies of the American churches have been toward the removal of the old ecclesiastical landmarks and of the denominational fences, a body which combats the liberalizing unification ideas of the times, believing in a unity of church forces only where there is an agreement on Biblical doctrines and practices, should have been able to mold the destinies of a mighty Church to the extent to which the Missourians have those of the Lutheran communion in this country....

Undoubtedly this pronounced conservative tendency in the Lutheran Church of the land is not solely due to the influence of the Missouri Synod, yet it has been the chief agency."

According to the statistics of 1918, the Missouri Synod numbered: Baptized members, 1,100,000; communicants, 622,000; congregations in actual membership with Synod, 2,061; congregations served by pastors of Synod, but not in actual membership, 1,183; preaching-stations (at which no organization has as yet been effected), 1,002; pastors, 2,403; parochial schools, 1,846, with 1,050 male and 320 female teachers (besides these, 973 pastors are engaged in teaching in these schools), and 84,830 pupils; Sunday-school scholars, 92,316; two theological seminaries, having 13 professors and an enrolment of over 550 students; two teachers' seminaries or normal schools, with 22 teachers and 343 students; seven colleges, having a total of 54 instructors and 1,028 students.

The second member of the Synodical Conference is the Joint Synod of Wisconsin, Minnesota, Michigan, and Other States. Originally these were three independent synods, but in order to be able to carry on their work more effectually, they united into a general body in 1892. Before the union each synod had its own theological seminary—the Wisconsin Synod at Milwaukee, the Minnesota Synod at New Ulm, Minn., and the Michigan Synod at Saginaw, Mich. The seminary at Milwaukee was retained by the general body, that of New Ulm was changed into a normal school for the education of parochial schoolteachers, that of Saginaw into a preparatory school. Besides, the

Synod maintains a college, Northwestern University, at Watertown, Wis. The Joint Synod carries on home-mission work chiefly in the North Central States and a mission among the Indians of the Southwest.—Its publishing concern, the Northwestern Publishing House, is at Milwaukee. Its synodical organs are: *Das Gemeindeblatt,* the *Northwestern Lutheran,* and *Theologische Quartalschrift.* In doctrine as well as in practice the Joint Synod of Wisconsin, Minnesota, Michigan, and Other States is in complete harmony with the Missouri Synod.

Statistics of the Joint Synod of Wisconsin, Minnesota, Michigan, and Other States: Baptized members, 259,412; communicants, 199,670; congregations, 516; pastors, 428; number of parochial schools, 571, having 252 teachers (the rest of the schools are taught by pastors) and 36,052 pupils; number of Sunday-schools, 637, with 2,831 officers and teachers and 109,462 scholars. The Synod maintains one theological seminary with 4 professors and 42 students; one college with 15 instructors and 203 students, and one normal school, having 8 teachers and 93 students.

The third member of the Synodical Conference is the young Slovak Synod, organized in the year 1902 under the auspices of the Missouri Synod, which originally began and supported the work among these immigrants. The Slovaks are a Slavic race, closely related to the Bohemians. Their home is in the northern part of Hungary, whence, like many of the other races of Central and Southern Europe, they have begun to emigrate to our country in considerable numbers during late years.

The majority of them are Roman Catholics, but not a few were won for the Lutheran Church during the early spread of the Reformation in that section of Europe, and these Lutheran Slovak immigrants to our country are now being gathered within the fold of this young synod.

Statistics of the Slovak Synod: Baptized membership, 12,970; communicant, 8,570; congregations, 79; pastors, 30; parochial schools, 30, with 1,614 pupils, taught by 6 teachers and 24 pastors; 60 Sunday-schools, having 190 officers and teachers and 3,817 scholars. The Synod has no educational institutions of its own as yet. Its pastors and teachers are educated in the institutions of the Missouri Synod.[1]

THE UNITED LUTHERAN CHURCH

On April 18, 1917, at Philadelphia, the Joint Quadri-centennial Committee, appointed by the General Synod, the General Council, and the United Synod in the South to arrange for a union celebration of the Reformation, decided that the merging of the three affiliated general bodies would be "the fittest commemoration and noblest memorial of the four-hundredth Reformation Jubilee." Accordingly, the presidents of these bodies, being present, were requested to form a joint committee, which should prepare a constitution for a united Church and present the same to the three general bodies for their

---

[1] Editor's note: The synodical conference no longer exists, but the Missouri Synod and the Wisconsin Evangelical Lutheran Synod continue within this tradition.

consideration, and, if approved, for submission to the District Synods. The constitution framed by the committee was in the same year adopted by all of the three general bodies, the General Synod, which, in 1820, had been founded for the express purpose of uniting all Lutheran synods in America, being the first to assent to the merger during its session at Chicago, June 20 to 27, 1917. The various District Synods also having approved of the union and having ratified the constitution, the merger was consummated at New York City, November 15, 1918. Dr. F. H. Knubel, a member of the General Synod, was elected President of the new body—"The United Lutheran Church in America." Of the total number of Lutherans in America (63 synods, 15,243 congregations, 9,790 pastors, 2,450,000 confirmed and 3,780,000 baptized members) the United Church embraces 45 synods, 10 theological seminaries with 46 professors and 267 students, 17 colleges, 6 academies, 3,747 congregations and mission-posts, 2,754 pastors, almost 1,000,000 baptized members, and 758,000 confirmed members, the General Synod contributing 364,000, the General Council 340,000, and the United Synod in the South 53,000. The United Church is the second largest Lutheran body in America, the Synodical Conference outnumbering it by only about 50,000 confirmed members. In 1919 it was decided to consolidate the *Lutheran*, the *Lutheran Church Work and Observer*, and the *Lutheran Church Visitor*. The name of the new official church-paper is *The Lutheran*.

The official doctrinal basis of the "United Lutheran Church in America" reads as follows:

"Article II. Section 1. The United Lutheran Church in America receives and holds the canonical Scriptures of the Old and New Testaments as the inspired Word of God, and as the only infallible rule and standard of faith and practice, according to which all doctrines and teachers are to be judged. Section 2. The United Lutheran Church in America accepts the three ecumenical creeds: namely, the Apostles', the Nicene, and the Athanasian, as important testimonies drawn from the Holy Scriptures, and rejects all errors which they condemn. Section 3. The United Lutheran Church in America receives and holds the Unaltered Augsburg Confession as a correct exhibition of the faith and doctrine of the Evangelical Lutheran Church, founded upon the Word of God; and acknowledges all churches that sincerely hold and faithfully confess the doctrines of the Unaltered Augsburg Confession to be entitled to the name of Lutheran. Section 4. The United Lutheran Church in America recognizes the Apology of the Augsburg Confession, the Smalcald Articles, the Large and Small Catechisms of Luther, and the Formula of Concord as in the harmony of one and the same pure Scriptural faith."

According to its constitution the United Lutheran Church it not merely an advisory, but a legislative body. That is to say, its resolutions are binding on the District Synods and their congregations. Article III, Section 6, of the constitution provides: "Congregations representatively constituting the various synods may elect delegates through their synods to represent them in a general body, all decisions of which, when made in accordance with the constitution, *bind*, so far as the terms of mutual agreement make them binding, those congregations and synods which consent to be represented in the general body."

The United Lutheran Church was not born of true inner unity in the Spirit and complete Lutheran loyalty, but of the desire for external union despite the lack of real and entire agreement in the truth. Its churchly character is not genuinely Lutheran, but indifferentistic and unionistic. This appears from the actual conditions as to Lutheran doctrine and practice generally prevailing within the synods composing the new body. It is indifferentistic with respect to the manifold deviations from the Lutheran symbols in its own midst, as well as within other Lutheran synods in America. According to Article III, Section 7, of its constitution the United Lutheran Church assumes responsibility only for the official doctrine and practice of the District Synods as such, not for what individual congregations, pastors, or laymen may teach and practice. Nor has the new body taken a clear and firm stand against the lodges and against altar- and pulpit-fellowship, and all manner of religious cooperation with the sects. This non-committal attitude was the chief reason why the Augustana Synod, the Iowa Synod, and the Ohio Synod declined to join the Merger. Thus the actual confessional position of the United Lutheran Church is not at all in agreement with its official doctrinal basis. Its Lutheranism does not rise above the doctrinal and practical level of the three uniting bodies before the merger: the General

Synod, the General Council, and the United Synod in the South.

The General Synod was organized October 22, 1820, at Hagerstown, Md., by four synods—the Ministerium of Pennsylvania, the Ministerium of New York, the Synod of North Carolina, and that of Maryland and Virginia. During its early years the new body had somewhat rough sailing. Two of these synods soon withdrew again, and during the first ten years of its existence growth was slow. Then followed a period of rapid development, extending from 1831 until the time of the Civil War. At the end of that period the General Synod comprised 26 synods, with 1,313 pastors and 164,000 communicant members. The whole Lutheran Church in the United States at that time numbered about 245,000 communicants, so that the General Synod comprised approximately two-thirds of the entire number of Lutherans in the country. The next ten years formed another period of loss. During the War the Southern synods withdrew, and in, and after, 1866 a number of Northern synods left to form the General Council.

By far the greater part of the work of the synods which constituted the General Synod is done in English, only two of these synods (the Wartburg and Nebraska Synods) being preponderatingly German. They maintain six theological seminaries, *viz.*, at Hartwick, N.Y., Gettysburg and Selinsgrove, Pa., Springfield, O., Atchison, Kans., and Lincoln, Nebr. A seminary is also supported at Breklum, Germany. Besides this they have a number of colleges and eleemosynary institutions in different sections of the country, and missions in India and in Liberia, Africa. Their chief periodicals before the merger were: *The Lutheran Quarterly*, the *Lutheran Church Work and Observer*, and the German organ *Lutherische Zionsbote*.

The 1918 statistics of the General Synod give the following data: Baptized members, 474,740; communicant members, 364,072; congregations, 1,857; pastors, 1,450; parochial schools, none; Sunday-schools, 1,772; officers and teachers, 29,717; pupils, 291,208. It has six theological seminaries with 27 professors and 145 students, and five colleges with 147 teachers and 2,406 students.

The original constitution of the General Synod contained no confessional paragraph. Later a formula was adopted, stating "that the fundamental doctrines of the divine Word are taught in a manner substantially correct in the twenty-one doctrinal articles of the Augsburg Confession." The doctrinal basis of the General Synod, officially adopted 1913 at Atchison, Kans., reads as follows: "Article II. With the Evangelical Lutheran Church of the Fathers, the General Synod receives and holds the canonical Scriptures of the Old and New Testaments as the Word of God, and the only infallible rule of faith and practice; and it receives and holds the Unaltered Augsburg Confession as a correct exhibition of the faith and doctrine of our Church as founded upon that Word. Article III. While the General Synod regards the Augsburg Confession as a sufficient and altogether adequate doctrinal basis for the cooperation of Lutheran synods, it also recognizes the Apology of the Augsburg Confession, the Smalcald Articles, the Small Catechism of Luther, the Large Catechism of Luther, and the Formula of Concord as expositions of Lutheran doctrine of great historical and interpretative value, and especially commends the Small Catechism as a book of instruction."

However, the actual conditions within the General Synod, before as well as after 1913, were in glaring conflict with the Lutheran Confessions adopted officially. Its doctrinal and practical position has always been a very liberal one. Many of its members held and openly advocated the Reformed doctrines on the Lord's Supper, Baptism, Absolution, the person of Christ, the Sabbath, temperance, etc. Pulpit- and altar-fellowship with other Protestant churches was freely indulged in by practically all of its District Synods and congregations. Nor did the General Synod ever take a stand against lodges. Even some of the most prominent of its ministers and officers were Freemasons.

The "General Council of the Evangelical Lutheran Church of America" owes its origin to the desire of a number of synods for a more conservative Lutheranism than was to be found in the General Synod. The prime mover in organizing the new body was the Ministerium of Pennsylvania. Immediately upon its withdrawal from the General Synod, in 1866, the Ministerium issued a call to other synods for a convention to organize a new general body. As a result, representatives of thirteen Lutheran synods met at Reading, Pa., where the "Fundamental Principles," formulated by C. P. Krauth, were adopted as a basis of organization. The first regular convention of the General Council was held 1867 at Fort Wayne, Ind. Only six of the original synods continued their connection with the Council, but in the course of years seven smaller synods were added. The largest and most important synods connected with the General Council were the Pennsylvania Synod, the New York Ministerium, the Pittsburgh Synod, and the Swedish Augustana Synod. Unwilling to join the United Lutheran Church, the last-named synod withdrew from the Council in 1918. Apart from the Augustana Synod the work of most of the synods which constituted the General Council is done in the English language. There are a number of German and German-English congregations, which, however, are rapidly becoming Americanized.

The synods connected with the General Council support the following theological seminaries: Philadelphia Seminary, at Mount Airy, Pa.; Chicago Seminary, at Maywood, Ill.; Augustana Seminary, at Rock Island, Ill. (belonging to the Swedish Augustana Synod); the seminary at Waterloo, Ont., Can. Financial aid is extended also to the seminary at Kropp, Germany. Besides these they maintain six colleges and higher institutions of learning, numerous charitable institutions, and a flourishing mission in India.

Among the prominent and representative men belonging to the synods which shaped the destinies of the General Council the foremost is Henry Melchior Muhlenberg, who has been called the "Patriarch of the Lutheran Church in America."

He was the father of the Pennsylvania Synod, which, in turn, became the founder of the Council. Muhlenberg was born in Germany in 1711, where he received his theological training. He came to America in 1742 and began his work among the neglected Lutheran congregations in Pennsylvania, but extended his activity as far south as Georgia. Although of pietistic and unionistic leanings, Muhlenberg no doubt did a great pioneer work among the scattered Lutherans of the American colonies. He died in 1787.

The most influential theologian of the General Council was Charles Porterfield Krauth (born 1823, died 1883). He wrote the *Fundamental Principles* mentioned above; was professor in the theological seminary at Philadelphia from 1864 until his death; edited *The Lutheran and Missionary*, later *The Lutheran*, from 1861; was president of the Council from 1870 to 1880. His best-known book is *The Conservative Reformation and Its Theology*, which appeared in 1872. Raised and educated in the General Synod, he entertained distinctly liberal principles in his earlier years, but with ripening age became more and more conservative.

The 1918 statistical report of the General Council (exclusive of the Augustana Synod) gives the following numbers: Baptized members, 482,108; communicant members, 340,588; congregations, 1,406; pastors, 1,059; parochial schools (mostly Saturday-and vacation-schools), 160, with 149 teachers and 7,343 pupils (the remainder presumably taught by pastors); Sunday-schools, 1,331, with 19,969 officers and teachers and 211,580 pupils. It maintains 4 theological seminaries with

19 professors and 123 students, and 8 colleges and academies with 75 instructors and 961 pupils.

The confessional basis of the General Council is stated in the *Fundamental Principles* as follows: "Art. VIII. We accept and acknowledge the doctrines of the Unaltered Augsburg Confession in its original sense, as throughout in conformity with the pure truth of which God's Word is the only rule. We accept its statements of truth as in perfect accordance with the canonical Scriptures. We reject the errors it condemns, and believe that all which it commits to the liberty of the Church of right belongs to that liberty.—Art. IX. In thus formally accepting and acknowledging the Unaltered Augsburg Confession, we declare our conviction that the other Confessions of the Evangelical Lutheran Church, inasmuch as they set forth none other than its system of doctrine and articles of faith, are of necessity pure and Scriptural."

However, the actual conditions within the General Council have never been in keeping with its official declarations. In reality the Council was an indifferentistic and unionistic body, though not in the same degree as the General Synod. On the so-called Four Points: altar-fellowship, pulpit-fellowship, lodges, and Chiliasm, the attitude of the General Council was never in agreement with the Lutheran Confessions. It tolerated all manner of fellowship and cooperation with the sects, membership in lodges, even on the part of some of its ministers and church officers, and various doctrinal aberrations from the Lutheran symbols on the part of her pastors, professors and editors.

As in the General Synod, so also in the Council parochial schools were not fostered to any extent.

The United Synod in the South came into existence, at least indirectly, in consequence of the sectional feeling engendered between the North and the South by the Civil War. The four Southern synods which had until that time belonged to the General Synod, *viz.*, the South Carolina, North Carolina, Virginia, and Southwest Virginia Synods, withdrew in 1863, and, together with the Georgia Synod, organized the "General Synod of the Evangelical Lutheran Church in the Confederate States of America." After the downfall of the Confederacy, at the close of the War, this name was changed to "The Evangelical Lutheran General Synod in North America," and still later into "The General Synod of the Evangelical Lutheran Church in the South."

One important Southern synod, the Tennessee Synod, founded in 1820, at first stood aloof from this union for confessional reasons, just as it had before the war refrained, for the same reason, from joining the northern General Synod. In 1867, however, Tennessee opened negotiations with the northern general body, looking towards a union with it. But not until 1884 did these negotiations lead to the adoption of a satisfactory doctrinal basis by delegates from the Tennessee Synod and the synods connected with the General Synod South assembled in a diet or colloquium at Salisbury, N. C. This basis was ratified in 1886 by the general body at Roanoke, Va., and the outcome was the organization of the present "United Synod of the Ev. Luth. Church in the South." The new general body accepted the Lutheran symbols contained in the Book of Concord of 1580 "as true and faithful developments of the doctrines taught in the Augsburg Confession, and in the perfect harmony of one and the same pure Scriptural faith." However, despite this official declaration, the United Synod in the South has in reality always been indifferentistic and unionistic. It tolerated pulpit-and altar-fellowship with the sects. And a number of their ministers were lodge-members. As to Lutheran doctrine and practice, it occupied a middle ground between the General Synod and the General Council.

The work of the synods connected with the United Synod in the South is almost exclusively carried on in the English language. Their theological seminary is located at Columbia, S. C. Besides, they maintain several coeducational colleges, and seminaries for females only. Their publishing house is at Columbia, S. C. Their official organ was the *Lutheran Church Visitor.* They carry on a mission in Japan. Prominent among their pastors were Dr. Bachmann, the first president of the General Synod in the South, Dr. Bittle, the first secretary, and in the Tennessee Synod, the Henkel family, which during several generations furnished preachers that were in the vanguard of confessional Lutheranism in America.

The 1918 statistical report of the United Synod gives the following data: Baptized members, 73,510; communicant members, 53,226, congregations, 484; pastors 257; no parochial schools; number of Sunday-schools, 429; officers and teachers, 4,305; pupils, 38,552. There are in the bounds of the United Synod one theological seminary with 3 professors and 14 students, 3 colleges with 51 teachers and 694 students.[2]

INDEPENDENT LUTHERAN SYNODS

THE OHIO SYNOD

During the closing decades of the eighteenth century numerous Lutheran immigrants moved westward from Pennsylvania and Virginia to the territory now embraced in the State of Ohio. In 1805 the Ministerium of Pennsylvania began to send out ministers to serve these Lutherans. These met in a special conference in 1812, and organized as a general conference at Somerset, O., in 1818, and in 1830 assumed the name of "Ev. Luth. Synod of Ohio and Adjacent States." The first meeting of the Joint Synod was held at Zelienople, Pa., in 1833. During the first decades of its existence as conference and then as synod, the body was permeated by the same spirit of liberalism that pervaded the General Synod. In the course of time, however, a more positive and confessional tendency set in, due in large measure to its contact with the Missouri Synod. In 1848 resolutions were adopted accepting all the Lutheran Symbols as binding. In consequence of its confessional progress the Ohio Synod refused to join the

---

[2] Editor's note: In 1962, the ULC joined the Lutheran Church in America, which was one of the synods who later formed the Evangelical Lutheran Church in America. Many of these congregations have since joined the North American Lutheran Church and the Lutheran Churches in Mission for Christ.

General Council at the organization of that body in 1867, but became a member of the Synodical Conference in 1871. Ten years later, 1881, the Joint Synod of Ohio, falsely charging Dr. Walther and the Missouri Synod with Calvinism, severed its connection with the Synodical Conference. The controversy between the two synods, especially on the doctrines of conversion and election, has as yet not been settled. For the last forty years representative theologians of the Ohio Synod have maintained: The reason why some are converted and finally saved, while the rest are lost, is, because their conduct toward God's grace is not as bad, and hence their guilt is not as great, as that of those who are lost. Rejecting this teaching as synergism, Missouri maintains: The reason why some are elected, converted, and finally saved is in every respect the grace of God alone; and the reason why some are lost is in every respect the perverted will of man alone. Like the synods in the Synodical Conference, Ohio fosters the parochial school and lays stress upon thorough instruction of the young in the catechism. It is, like them, also opposed to secret societies, though probably in both these matters it is less zealous than the aforementioned synods.

The work of the Ohio Synod is bilingual, being about equally divided between German and English, and extends through a number of the North Central and Western States. Its main theological ("theoretical") seminary is at Columbus, O.; besides this it has a "practical" seminary at St. Paul, Minn., and at Olympia, Wash. Its chief colleges are Capital University at

Columbus, O., and the normal school at Woodville, O. Its publishing house is also at Columbus. The synodical organs are the *Lutherische Kirchenzeitung* and the *Lutheran Standard*, and for preachers it publishes the *Theological Magazine*, combined with *Theologische Zeitblaetter.*—It conducts mission-work in Africa. Profs. Lehmann, Loy, and Stellhorn were among the leading theologians of the Ohio Synod.

Statistics of the Ohio Synod: Baptized membership, 204,583; communicant, 138,542; congregations, 916; pastors, 685; parochial schools, 281, with 140 teachers (the rest of the schools are taught by pastors) and 9,895 pupils; the number of Sunday-schools is 729, with 4,513 officers and teachers and 64,055 pupils. The synod maintains 3 theological seminaries with 11 professors and 74 students, and three colleges with 32 teachers and 329 students.

THE BUFFALO SYNOD

Numerically this synod is one of the minor Lutheran bodies, but historically it has played a rather prominent role. It was founded in 1845 by a number of Lutheran congregations and ministers who had emigrated from different parts of Germany during the preceding years under the leadership of Rev. J. A. A. Grabau and Captain H. von Rohr, in order to escape from the religious persecution to which they had been subjected there. The synod takes its name from the circumstance that its oldest congregation and its college is located in the city of Buffalo, N. Y., and its official organ is also published there. Its recognized leader from the beginning was Pastor Grabau. He harbored hierarchical principles, which soon brought him into a conflict with Walther and the Missouri Synod, who upheld the rights of the spiritual priesthood of all Christians. The controversy led to a disruption in the Buffalo Synod in 1866. Only a few of the pastors and congregations remained faithful to Grabau, the remainder entering into negotiations with the Missouri Synod and, after reaching an agreement with it regarding the disputed points, uniting with that synod. In 1919 the Buffalo Synod entered into church-fellowship with the Iowa Synod.

The doctrinal position of Pastor Grabau, who died in 1879, may be summarized as follows: The Church (meaning the One Holy Christian Church of the Third Article) is essentially visible, being embodied in the Lutheran Church, which, therefore, is the only saving Church. Where the Gospel is not taught in entire purity, there can be no Church. To gain salvation it is not sufficient to belong to the invisible Church, but it is necessary to be a member of the visible Church. The office of the keys, *i. e.*, the power to remit and retain sins, was given to the clergy alone, not to lay-Christians. The office of the ministry is not conferred by the congregations. Ordination was instituted by God. Communion, when administered by a pastor without a legitimate call, is no sacrament. Also in matters not commanded in God's Word a congregation owes obedience to its pastor. Not the congregations, but the ministerium of synod is the tribunal to judge doctrine and practice of the pastors; therefore congregations are bound to obtain, and abide by, the advice of the ministerium.—With regard to the doctrine of conversion and election the Buffalo Synod later sided with the Ohio Synod.

Statistics of the Buffalo Synod: Baptized membership, 9,379; communicants, 7,395; congregations, 49; pastors, 36; no statistics on parochial schools are available; Sunday-schools (as given by the *Year Book of Churches for 1918*), 23, with 176 teachers and officers and 1,524 pupils; 1 theological seminary with 3 professors and 7 students.

THE IOWA SYNOD

This synod was founded in 1854 at St. Sebald, near Dubuque, Iowa, by four ministers and one layman, chiefly at the instigation of Pastor William Loehe, a noted Lutheran theologian of Germany, who had previously worked in harmony with the Missouri Synod, but later, on account of several doctrinal differences which had developed between him and that synod, turned away from it, and now encouraged the organization of this new synod for the promulgation of his tenets in America. During succeeding years Loehe sent over quite a number of ministers to reinforce the new body, which was at first very weak numerically. In 1855 Pastor Grabau, the leader of the Buffalo Synod, came West to seek an understanding with the Iowans. In this he was successful; but the relation between the two synods lasted for a short while only because of the position which the Iowa Synod assumed with reference to Chiliasm and the Lutheran Symbols. Eleven years later, in 1866, when the Pennsylvania Synod issued its call for the formation of a new body, which resulted in the organization of the General Council, the Iowa Synod resolved to join this body. But on account of the non-committal position of the Council towards lodges and pulpit- and altar-fellowship, it declined to consummate the union in the following year. However, while not organically united with the Council, it remained in virtual fellowship with it, sending an advisory delegate to its meetings, and cooperating with it also in foreign mission-work.

Efforts to effect an agreement between Iowa and Missouri resulted in a "colloquium," which was held 1867 between leading men of both synods at Milwaukee. But the desired unity failed of realization. What Missouri objected to was the attitude of the Iowa Synod especially toward the so-called "Open Questions," Chiliasm, the Antichrist, and Ordination. A pro-Missouri movement within the Iowa Synod, which followed the "colloquium," finally (in 1875) resulted in the withdrawal of some 20 of its pastors. In the Predestination controversy Iowa sided with Ohio, with which, as also with the Buffalo Synod, complete church-fellowship was established in 1919.

The work of the Iowa Synod was at first almost entirely in German, but has become largely bilingual from the same causes that operate in the other originally German synods. Its theological seminary, after several removals, is now located at Dubuque, Iowa, its main college is at Clinton,

Iowa, and its normal school at Waverly, Iowa. Besides these it supports several other institutions of higher education. The Wartburg Publishing House has branches in Chicago and Waverly. It publishes *Kirchenblatt, Kirchliche Zeitschrift*, and several smaller periodicals.—In its early years it began a mission among the Indians of the West, but untoward circumstances, notably the hostility of the Indians themselves and their going upon the warpath, caused the suspension of the work, which has not been resumed. Among the leaders of the Iowa Synod Sigmund and Gottfried Fritschel, Grossmann, and Deindoerfer occupy the first place.

Statistics of the Iowa Synod: Number of baptized members, 197,720; communicant members, 125,458; congregations, 1,056; pastors, 576; parochial schools, 830; teachers, 65 (the remainder of schools taught by pastors); pupils, 15,541; Sunday-schools, 1,036; teachers and officers, 2,957; pupils, 32,209; 1 theological seminary with 4 professors and 48 students, and two colleges with 20 teachers and 232 students.[3]

THE SWEDISH AUGUSTANA SYNOD

The Swedes began to immigrate into this country in large numbers about the middle of the

---

[3] Editor's note: The Iowa Synod, Ohio Synod, and Buffalo Synod eventually became founding churches of the American Lutheran Church in 1960. Most of these congregations joined the Evangelical Lutheran Church in America. Some congregations resisted this merger and now exist as the Association of American Lutheran Churches.

last century. In the year 1850 a Swedish Lutheran congregation was organized at Andover, Ill., and a little later others were founded at Galesburg and Moline, Ill., as well as at New Sweden, Iowa, and preaching-stations were established at other places, all served by the Rev. L. P. Esbjörn. These, together with five Norwegian Lutheran congregations of Northern Illinois, the following year formed "The Ev. Luth. Synod of Northern Illinois."

Meanwhile the Scandinavians began to flock into the country in ever greater numbers, and to invade the neighboring States, particularly Minnesota, and with their increase in numbers grew the sentiment in favor of the organization of a distinctively Scandinavian Lutheran synod. And thus representatives of the various Scandinavian conferences met at Clinton, Wis., in 1860, the outcome of which was the formation of "The Scandinavian Ev. Luth. Augustana Synod of North America," numbering 49 congregations, 4,967 communicants, and 27 pastors. An institution for the education of pastors, Augustana Seminary, was at once founded and located at Chicago, from where it was later removed to Paxton, Ill., and thence to Rock Island, Ill. In 1870 the Norwegians withdrew, in order to form their own synod, so that the Augustana Synod now became distinctively Swedish. At that time the Swedish part reported 99 congregations, 16,376 communicants, and 46 ministers. Swedish immigration steadily increased during these years and scattered the nationality broadcast over the country, particularly the Northwest, and into

Canada, and naturally the work of the synod became enlarged and extended in proportion.

In doctrine and practice the Augustana Synod occupies the same position as did the General Council, to which it belonged until 1918. Its churchly character was pietistic and indifferentistic. Answering the question, "What are the special characteristics of the Augustana Synod?" in the *Lutheran Encyclopedia*, Prof. Olson, of the Augustana Synod, says: "The old pietistic confessionalism and churchliness of the Swedish people, the Evangelicalism of the Church of Sweden. From the beginning until now every candidate for the ministry has been asked in the ministerium what he has to say about his personal spiritual experience of his inmost heart during his past life and at the present time. Unfeigned orthodoxy [?], personal piety, sincere spiritual and moral life have so far been expected and required in a pastor by our congregations. Against an ungodly life of church-members our constitution for the congregations takes a firm stand, and the pastor and church council are solemnly charged with the duty of pastoral care of young and old members of the church. Thorough catechetical instruction in the confirmation class is held to be the most sacred and blessed duty of a pastor in our Church. Against secret societies our constitutions have fought from the beginning."

Statistics of the Augustana Synod: Baptized membership, 278,333; communicants, 191,390; congregations, 1,225; pastors, 720; parochial (vacation) schools, 450, with 598 teachers and 17,263 pupils; Sunday-schools, 1,200, with 12,000 officers and 817,264 scholars. The Synod maintains one theological seminary with 6 professors and 101 students, and 8 colleges and academies, having a total of 189 instructors and 3,193 pupils.

THE UNITED (NORWEGIAN) LUTHERAN SYNOD IN AMERICA

On June 9, 1917, in a meeting held at Minneapolis, Minn., the three largest Norwegian Lutheran synods, the Hauge Synod, the Synod for the Norwegian Lutheran Church, and the United Norwegian Lutheran Church, were consolidated in one body under the name which stands at the head of this section. Preliminary negotiations looking towards this union had been carried on for a number of years previously, in order to clear away some differences in doctrine and practice that existed among the three bodies, and the union was finally effected by the adoption, on the part of the three uniting bodies, of the so-called "Opgjör," a unionistic and synergistic document. By the union the three bodies were merged into one, thus ceasing to exist as individual synods. Accordingly, all the work which had been done individually by the three synods is now carried on by the one body, and all the property of the three bodies, both at home and in mission-fields, was transferred to it. The three theological seminaries which had been maintained by the three synods were also merged into one. The new body was divided into nine districts, and its numerical strength is shown by the following table.

Statistics: Baptized membership, 443,563; communicants, 276,000 (approximate figures); congregations, 2,811; pastors, 1,240; parochial schools (mostly Saturday and vacation-schools), 853, with 1,283 instructors and 50,371 pupils; Sunday-schools, 964, with 5,664 officers and teachers and 46,885 scholars; 1 theological seminary with 10 professors, 1 proseminary, 4 colleges having 66 teachers and 1,180 students.

Hauge's Norwegian Ev. Luth. Synod in America took its name from Hans Nielson Hauge, a lay-preacher of a pietistical and methodistical turn of mind, who labored in Norway and Denmark at the beginning of the last century against the prevailing rationalism that had come over into the Scandinavian countries from Germany. One of his followers, the lay-preacher Elling Eielson, came to this country and during the early forties collected the "awakened," as the followers of Hauge styled themselves, into congregations. These congregations, in 1846, formed a loose organization, but not until 1874 did they organize themselves formally into a synod by adopting a new constitution and the name which stands at the head. Eielson, with a number of adherents, afterwards, withdrew from this reorganized body because of its "high-churchism," and with them returned to their old constitution. The Synod, since 1879, maintained a college at Red Wing, Minn., for the education of its ministers and teachers. Another college was owned and controlled by the Iowa District of the synod. The synod also supported an orphan home and owned a printing establishment. Its official paper was

Budbaereren. In addition to its home mission-work it carried on a mission in China. The character of Hauge's Synod has always been unionistic and pietistic in doctrine and practice. Statistics: Members, 29,893; congregations, 363; pastors, 121; Sunday-schools, 301, with 1,575 officers and teachers and 14,011 pupils.

The Synod for the Norwegian Ev. Luth. Church in America was organized in 1853 by seven pastors, who served about forty congregations. It early entered into church-fellowship with the Missouri Synod, and for a number of years its ministers were educated at Concordia Seminary, St. Louis. From 1872 until 1883 it was a member of the Synodical Conference, leaving this body in the latter year, not on account of doctrinal differences, but for reasons of expediency. Until its recent amalgamation with the two other Norwegian synods it maintained a theological seminary at Minneapolis. Its official organ was *Ev. Luth. Kirketidende.* Among its leading men were H. A. Preuss, Dr. A. V. Koren, and Dr. L. Larsen. In 1916 it numbered 112,773 members, 981 congregations, 447 pastors, 465 Sunday-schools with 2,817 officers and teachers, and 24,313 scholars.

The United Norwegian Lutheran Church in America was founded in 1890 by the union of "The Conference for the Danish-Norwegian Church of America," "The Norwegian-Danish Augustana Synod," and the "Anti-Missourians," who had withdrawn from the Norwegian Synod in the controversy on conversion and predestination. Embodying in its membership the "anti-Missourian" faction under the leadership of Prof. F.

A. Schmidt, who, together with Prof. Stellhorn of the Ohio Synod, was one of the chief opponents of Dr. Walther in the predestinarian controversy, the United Norwegian Church, of course, occupied practically the same position as Ohio on this particular question, while on general principles its position was a liberal one in doctrine and practice. In 1916 the United Church embraced 177,463 members, 1,399 congregations, 598 pastors, 897 Sunday-schools with 5,787 teachers and officers, and 44,645 scholars.

THE NORWEGIAN SYNOD OF THE AMERICAN EV. LUTHERAN CHURCH

Soon after the Synod for the Norwegian Ev. Luth. Church in America had been merged in the United (Norwegian) Lutheran Synod in America, a portion of its membership, who had refused to join the new body "for conscience' sake," met at Lake Mills, Iowa (from June 14 to 19, 1918), for the purpose of reorganizing their synod. One of the first things they did was, by a rising and unanimous vote, to reaffirm their uncompromising stand upon the Holy Scriptures as the only foundation and standard of faith and practice and the interpretation of the same as contained in the Book of Concord. The name adopted was "The Norwegian Synod of the American Ev. Luth. Church." This synod occupies the same position as the Synodical Conference, and expects to become a member of this body at its next meeting.

THE NORWEGIAN LUTHERAN FREE CHURCH

The original nucleus of this organization were the so-called "Friends of Augsburg Seminary," a theological Norwegian institution located at Minneapolis, originally the property of the so-called "Conference," but since 1890 under the control of the United Norwegian Church. On account of the principles of this institution strong opposition against it developed after that date. In 1893 this led to the withdrawal of the above-named faction, whose members favor a pietistic education of ministers and loose synodical connection of congregations. It was not until 1897 that they organized under the above name. The Lutheran Free Church, which is unionistic and pietistic in character, is active in home mission, foreign mission, mission to the Jews, deaconess work, and other works of charity, and supports a theological seminary.

Statistics: Baptized members, 45,547; communicants, 20,536; congregations, 420; pastors, 198; parochial schools (Saturday-and vacation-schools), 200; teachers, 210; pupils, 6,000; Sunday-schools, 300; officers and teachers, 900; scholars, 10,000 (evidently these are estimates in round numbers); 1 theological seminary, with 4 professors and 21 students, and 1 college with 8 teachers and 28 students.[4]

THE DANISH EV. LUTHERAN CHURCH IN AMERICA

---

[4] Editor's note: The Lutheran Free Church joined with the ALC in 1962, and several congregations resisted this split. They exist today as the Association of Free Lutheran Congregations.

This synod was founded 1872 and formally organized 1878. Aside from its Grundtvigian position, according to which the authority of the Apostles' Creed is greater than that of the Bible, the Danish Church adopts the three Ecumenical Creeds, the Augsburg Confession, and Luther's Small Catechism. Statistics: Baptized members, 21,491; confirmed members, 14,463; congregations, 112; pastors, 74; parochial schools (chiefly Saturday-and vacation-schools), 84; teachers, 84; pupils, 2,230; Sunday-schools, 58; officers and teachers, 266; scholars, 2,570; 1 theological seminary with 3 professors and 14 students; 1 college having 10 teachers and 140 students.

THE UNITED DANISH EVANGELICAL LUTHERAN CHURCH IN AMERICA

This body resulted from a disruption of the Danish Church in 1894. The minority, opponents of the adherents of Grundtvig, withdrew and formed a union under the name of "The Danish Ev. Luth. Church in America." Two years later that body united with "The Danish Evangelical Association of America," a church-body of Danes that had been organized in 1884 by pastors and congregations that had been members of the Norwegian-Danish Church Conference. This newly formed organization took the name of "The United Danish Evangelical Church in America." Its congregations, mostly small and poor, are scattered from New York to California and from Oklahoma to Canada. It supports missions among the Mormons in Utah, the Indians in Oklahoma, and in Japan. It embraces 23,729 baptized and 14,996 communicant members, 185 congregations and 143 pastors; it has 185 Sunday-schools with 840 teachers and officers and 7,679 pupils; 1 theological seminary with 2 professors and 5 students, and 1 college with 11 teachers and 159 students. Doctrinally this body occupies about the same liberal position that the General Synod did.

THE ICELANDIC EV. LUTH. SYNOD OF AMERICA

The first Icelandic congregation was organized in northern Wisconsin in 1875 by the Rev. Paul Thorlakson, a graduate of Concordia Seminary, St. Louis. Other congregations were formed in Manitoba, 1877–78. In the following years a number of the Icelandic settlers moved from Canada to North Dakota, where a flourishing colony was started under the leadership of Thorlakson, who, however, died soon after. H. B. Thorgrimsen, another graduate of Concordia Seminary, St. Louis, took charge of the work in North Dakota. The Icelandic Synod, organized 1885 in Winnipeg, embraces a membership of 6,810 souls, 4,598 communicants, 55 congregations, and 16 pastors; its Sunday-schools number 33, with 190 officers and teachers and 1,756 scholars. In doctrine and practice this synod leans toward the General Council.

THE FINNISH SYNOD

Like their Scandinavian neighbors from the North of Europe, the Finns—who, by the way, like the Lapps and Eskimos, are classed with the Mongolian race—upon their immigration mostly settle in the northern part of our country. The Finnish Suomi Synod was organized and incorporated in the State of Michigan in the year 1890, and has enjoyed a steady growth ever since. It has 32,541 baptized and 16,511 communicant members, 151 congregations and 40 pastors, 61 parochial schools with 65 teachers and 3,998 pupils, and 185 Sunday-schools with 1,314 teachers and officers and 9,446 scholars; 1 theological seminary, with 2 professors and 8 students, and 1 college with 11 instructors and 127 pupils. The Finns occupy about the same position doctrinally as the Icelanders, leaning towards the General Council.

www.ingramcontent.com/pod-product-compliance
Lightning Source LLC
Chambersburg PA
CBHW072017040426
42447CB00009B/1659